POWERSHELL

WITHOUT THE

SHELL SHOCK

A Uniquely different approach

Richard Thomas Edwards

Introduction

Why Powershell

*This is not one of those stuffy books you only use
once and collects dust on your on your book shelf.*
—Richard Thomas Edwards

ou are an amazing person. Why shouldn't be reading a book that is just as
equally amazing?

A few years ago, I was in your position looking at this:

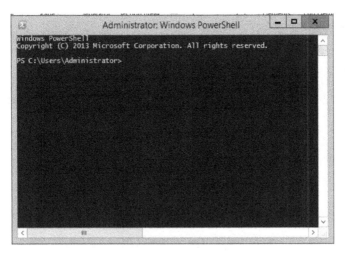

And wondering why I should even bother with another Microsoft product that appeared to be doing what all monopoly does best. Kill its competition.

So, who are you? What's your current job status?

1. Unemployed
2. Under Employed
3. Retiring?
4. Ex-Military
5. In the military but about to get discharged
6. Put off career mom
7. Put off career dad
8. Recently divorced
9. Suddenly single due to a loss of a spouse
10. Wanting a career change
11. Looking for a promotion
12. Wanting to learn Powershell as a personal achievement

I'm hoping to help all of you. And I know I haven't failed at doing so. (I read the last page first, I know how it ends.)

By the way, I too, had one of those moments when a pivotal decision and firm commitment to learn as much as possible changed my career and my life forever.

There was a time when I had no idea what I wanted to do with my life. Having 5 children, I knew the work I was doing wasn't paying for the type of life I wanted to provide them for. I also knew that the work I was doing was dangerous.

I needed a career change.

Is this where you are?

Then read on.

prerequisites

In order to get the most out of this book, you will need the following:

1. A computer that works
2. Know how to type

3. Know how to use the mouse
4. Know how to get to things on your computer – like the menu.
5. Know what a command prompt is
6. Be willing to type lines on the command line and see what it does
7. Have some sort version of Microsoft Office installed
8. Be willing to install trial software such as SQL Server.
9. Be willing to install Visual Studio 2017 Community Edition
10. Be willing to spend at least an hour a day learn PowerShell
11. Be willing to learn how to read PowerShell scripts
12. Be willing to do a lot of cutting and pasting

If you are willing and able to do all of the above then we have a statement of work the two of us can share.

MOTIVES

Unless you are my wife, without motives, roller pin or frying pan "accidents" involving one's skull doesn't happen just because you breathe oxygen.

Therefore, your motives for purchasing this book should be one of the following:

1. You want to learn PowerShell for your own personal reasons
2. You want to teach PowerShell to others.
3. You want a job and you think PowerShell is the best way to get one.
4. You have a job and was asked to build a PowerShell script.
5. You have a job but it buried you alive and you think PowerShell is your shovel of salvation.
6. You love working with your computer and want to know more about what it does
7. You don't start yelling at the technical support people when they ask you to do something.
8. You own or rent Office 365 and you want to customize it to suit your needs.
9. You already know PowerShell but would like to understand more so you can improve on your skills.
10. You hate having stuff on your computer when you have no idea what it does. (And are afraid to find out.)
11. You want the computer to do more than collect dust when you are at work.
12. You like to learn through trial and error.

Doing a lot of up and down bobbing of your head?

Let's get cracking – hopefully not on my head and start you on your next adventure.

So You want to learn Powershell

*Chapter Epigraph uses a quote or verse to
introduce the chapter and set the stage.*
—*Attribute the quote*

Someone once said that the best way to learn how to swim is to be thrown into the deep end of the pool.

We should eradicate that saying, that person's linage from the face of this planet!

Truth is, the lungs don't work well filled with bleach tainted water – that could also be partly you know what else might be there to – as way to introduce one to swimming 101.

Never-the-less, here I am doing exactly that to you without the drowning part.

So, you want to learn PowerShell.

Would it shock you if I told you that you don't have much of a learning curve when it comes to using it?

Is that even possibly true?

It is.

At least it is up until the time that you want to create scripts that turn PowerShell into a programming work horse.

You see, PowerShell itself, has tons of already built in programmed scripts called CmdLets and functions that Administrators need to get work done without little to no programming experience..

How do you know what these scripts are? Is there a way to find out what they can do? And, last but not least, is there a way to learn what is required of the user to get them to work?

To answer the first question, start the PowerShell window based console:

Find this ICON 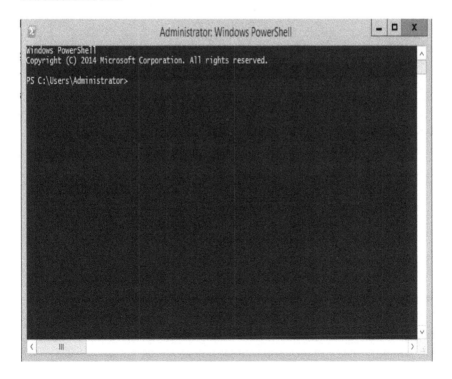 and click on it or go to start, run and type in PowerShell.

You should see this:

Your prompt might look a bit different but the PS line with a > is the prompt where you type in:

Get-Command

And then press enter.

In blazing fast speed, the console will fill the windows with all its capabilities.

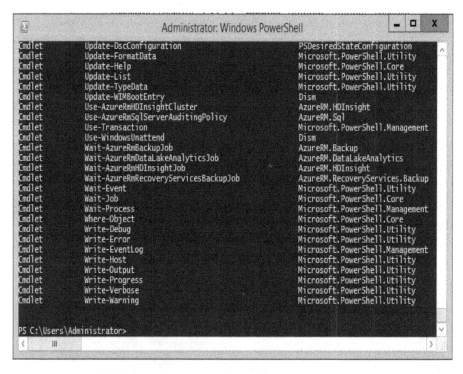

Since there is no way you can see or remember all of this, type:

Get-Command > C:\PowerShellCommands.txt

And press enter.

A file will be created in the C:\ directory and named PowerShellCommands.txt.

PowerShellCommands   8/7/2017 7:07 AM   Text Document

Okay, so that answered Question #1.

This should answer Question #2 and #3:

Say, I discovered there was a CmdLet called Get-WMIObject. To learn what it does and to find out how to use it, type:

Get-help Get-WMIObject -full

And press enter.

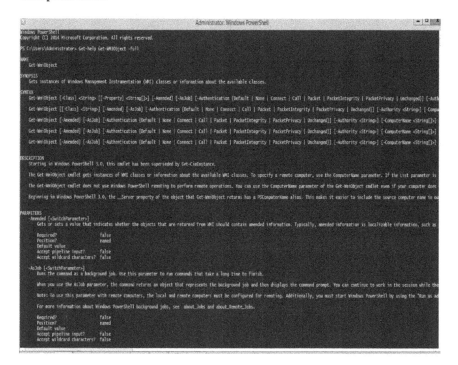

The first part of this screen provides you with a quick summary of what the CmdLet can do as well as the syntax you can use to make the command line work for you.

At the bottom of this are examples you can try:

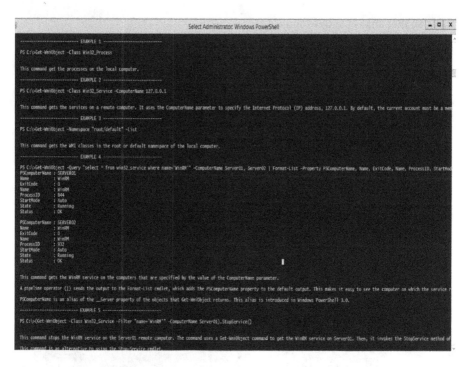

There are also related CmdLets:

```
Get-WSManInstance
Invoke-WSManAction
New-WSManInstance
Remove-WSManInstance
Invoke-WmiMethod
Remove-WmiObject
Set-WmiInstance
```

The very first example:

Get-WMIObject –class Win32_Process

And press enter, returns this:

```
                        Administrator: Windows PowerShell                          - □ X
Handle                : 6296
HandleCount           : 562
InstallDate           :
KernelModeTime        : 15312500
MaximumWorkingSetSize : 1380
MinimumWorkingSetSize : 200
Name                  : firefox.exe
OSCreationClassName   : Win32_OperatingSystem
OSName                : Microsoft Windows Server 2012 R2 Datacenter Evaluation|C:\Windows|\Device\Harddisk1\Partition4
OtherOperationCount   : 1441
OtherTransferCount    : 20196
PageFaults            : 147221
PageFileUsage         : 111860
ParentProcessId       : 7964
PeakPageFileUsage     : 134756
PeakVirtualSize       : 687128576
PeakWorkingSetSize    : 156648
Priority              : 8
PrivatePageCount      : 114544640
ProcessId             : 6296
QuotaNonPagedPoolUsage : 65
QuotaPagedPoolUsage   : 570
QuotaPeakNonPagedPoolUsage : 75
QuotaPeakPagedPoolUsage : 624
ReadOperationCount    : 19265
ReadTransferCount     : 65539845
SessionId             : 1
Status                :
TerminationDate       :
ThreadCount           : 64
UserModeTime          : 128593750
VirtualSize           : 653815808
WindowsVersion        : 6.3.9600
WorkingSetSize        : 141524992
WriteOperationCount   : 19116
WriteTransferCount    : 8588296
PSComputerName        : WIN-08PMHO8BTH1
ProcessName           : firefox.exe
Handles               : 562
VM                    : 653815808
WS                    : 141524992
Path                  : C:\Program Files (x86)\Mozilla Firefox\firefox.exe


PS C:\Users\Administrator>
```

That's a heck of a lot of information. You can also send it to a file like we did before (technically called pipe it out). Or you can filter for one specific property:

Try:

Get-WMIObject –class Win32_Process | select –Property Name

And press enter.

System Idle Process	System	smss.exe
csrss.exe	wininit.exe	csrss.exe
services.exe	lsass.exe	winlogon.exe

svchost.exe

atiesrxx.exe

svchost.exe

svchost.exe

svchost.exe

amdacpusrsvc.exe

horizon_client_service.exe

inetinfo.exe

SMSvcHost.exe

sqlwriter.exe

svchost.exe

vmware-usbarbitrator64.exe

svchost.exe

svchost.exe

conhost.exe

ftscanmgrhv.exe

vmwsprrdpwks.exe

regedit.exe

csrss.exe

dwm.exe

devenv.exe

conhost.exe

svchost.exe

svchost.exe

svchost.exe

wlanext.exe

svchost.exe

svchost.exe

svchost.exe

IpOverUsbSvc.exe

rxapi.exe

svchost.exe

wlms.exe

SMSvcHost.exe

WUDFHost.exe

WNDA3100v2.exe

SnagPriv.exe

msdtc.exe

WmiPrvSE.exe

armsvc.exe

winlogon.exe

rdpclip.exe

CodeBlue.vshost.exe

devenv.exe

dwm.exe

tbaseprovisioning.exe

svchost.exe

conhost.exe

spoolsv.exe

atieclxx.exe

ftnlsv.exe

mqsvc.exe

TCPSVCS.EXE

UploaderService.exe

WifiSvc.exe

svchost.exe

taskhostex.exe

Snagit32.exe

SnagitEditor.exe

svchost.exe

explorer.exe

splwow64.exe

LogonUI.exe

atieclxx.exe

IntelliTrace.exe

msvsmon.exe

Functions.vshost.exe	WINWORD.EXE	SnippingTool.exe
powershell.exe	conhost.exe	WmiPrvSE.exe
firefox.exe	firefox.exe	firefox.exe

I placed the names into a table much nicer to look at than a standard list taking up much more than a half page to show off.

Anyway, so the point to all of this is that PowerShell has the ability to provide you with what it expects you to know, so that you can type an intelligent request at the command line prompt.

To me, that makes PowerShell quite compelling.

How was your first swimming lesion?

The 12 most important facts about programming

You learn through trial and error, not by reading a book.
—Richard Thomas Edwards

The 12 most import facts about coding you will want to learn

There are 12 lines of code types used today in every language. These are:

1. The creation of an object
2. The use of a property to get\set a value
3. The use of a function that does or does not accept parameters and may or may not return a value. Functions are also called methods.
4. The use of an event that occurs and you write code to respond to it.
5. The use of enumerators
6. The use of conditional Loops
7. The use of conditional branches
8. The use of error trapping
9. Data Conversions
10. Constants
11. Declarations
12. Reg Expressions

It is your job – not mine – to find those patterns and apply them to your Powershell scripts.

What is Powershell

A s you already have had a your first swimming lesion experience and as the name suggests, is a console application that uses a command prompt to do all of its work.

That prompt, based on what directory PowerShell is being run from looks like this:

```
Windows PowerShell
Copyright (C) 2014 Microsoft Corporation. All rights reserved.

PS C:\Users\Administrator>
```

The three most important reasons why you would be interested in learning how to use PowerShell are below:

1. The most sophisticated programming tool you will ever use with the word **"FREE"** attached to it.
2. The most simplest to use, already installed, Administrator's tool on the market today.
3. The biggest pain in the butt to try to explain why you should use it!

SOME TECH TALK IN PLAIN ENGLISH

When someone says it comes in two flavors, they aren't talking ice cream. They are saying you have a choice between one way something will work and the other way something will work.

When someone says a 32bit operating system verses a 64bit operating system, the word that might be sprinkled into the conversation is "platform". As the name suggests, a platform is, real or imaginary, a way to allow other things to happen.

Both 32bit and 64bit operating systems are in themselves a platform because they allow or deny you the ability to run certain applications. For example, if you have a 32bit operating system, you can't run 64bit programs on them. But if you have a 64bit operating system. You can run both 34bit and 64bit programs on them.

Microsoft is well aware of this – since they built the operating system you are currently using and want to run PowerShell on it.

And on my menu after scrolling down to the bottom and expanding the view, I see these options available to me:

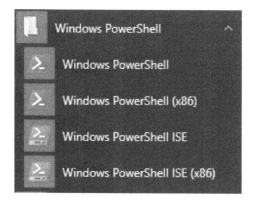

So, there are two versions of PowerShell and two versions of the ISE – where, when I get tired of seeing the same issue\solution repeats bedecked with dozens of ads around them – I come to so I can figure out the problem on my own. And keep a few more hairs on my head.

This is what the ISE looks like:

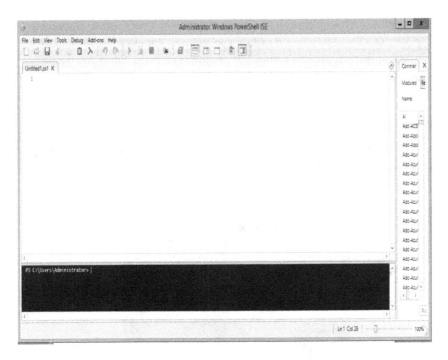

But it is just a tool used to get a job done. Another one of many tools you can use to perform similar tasks.

Where the real programming comes into play is when you know what you want to do that PowerShell doesn't know about or how to use.

That is what the rest of this book is all about.

How do you "break into" the workforce that employs PowerShell programmers?

Go to the various job sites that are on the internet and look at the jobs with their requirements.

Mold What you need to know based on Job Qualifications

I did a quick check on the types of jobs Dice you'll be able to do after finishing this book and it looks pretty good:

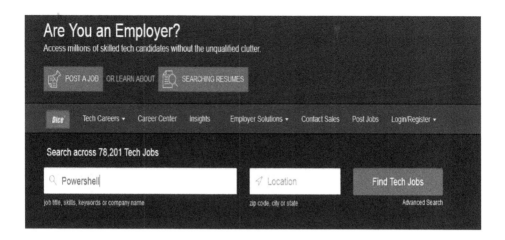

Powershell jobs

1 - 30 of 1,812 positions

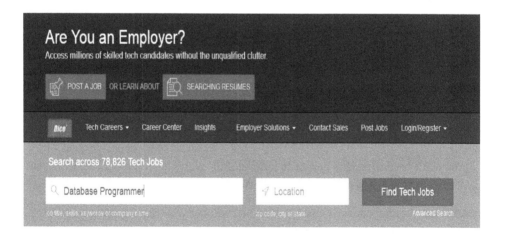

Database Programmer jobs

1 - 30 of 36,071 positions

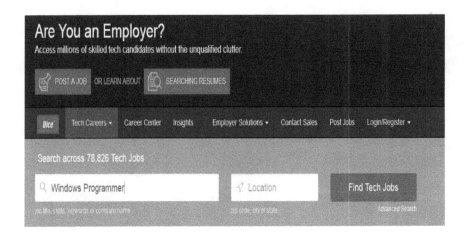

Windows Programmer jobs

1 - 30 of 36,396 positions

Making your work to learn Powershell much simpler

You don't need a learners permit to jump into the world of PowerShell. However, you may need some band aids for bruised egos.

First off, nothing happens inside PowerShell without you either running script or you typing something in and pressing enter.

So at that nonintrusive command prompt, type in your name and press enter.

Mine came out spitting red venom across my screen (which I can barely read):

PS C:\Users\Administrator> Richard T. Edwards

```
Richard : The term 'Richard' is not recognized as the name of a cmdlet, function, script file, or operable program. Check the spelling of
the name, or if a path was included, verify that the path is correct and try again.
At line:1 char:1
+ Richard T. Edwards
+ ~~~~~~~
    + CategoryInfo          : ObjectNotFound: (Richard:String) [], CommandNotFoundException
    + FullyQualifiedErrorId : CommandNotFoundException

PS C:\Users\Administrator>
```

PowerShell thought Richard should be the beginning of a command.

Now, press the up arrow on the keyboard. Your name returns! Okay, now, slide the cursor under the first letter of your name using the left arrow and click the shift and double quotes key. Slide the cursor to the very end of your last name and add a double quote there too.

Should Look like this.

"Richard T. Edwards"

And if you are having problems doing this, simply type over from the beginning of your name and add the quotes as you go. Once it looks like mine, press enter.

The response from PowerShell is:

```
PS C:\Users\Administrator> "Richard T. Edwards"
Richard T. Edwards
PS C:\Users\Administrator>
```

The reason why PowerShell didn't complain is because you entered a string and asked PowerShell to respond. So it returned with the string's value without the quotes around it.

There are three key commands:

1. Get-Command
2. Get-Help
3. Update-Help

The first one you should run is Update-Help.

This will update your help files.

Aside from that, I have created programs for you to help you lean PowerShell. I have included Windows based programs that will help you learn PowerShell. These include help viewers for CmdLets, Azure CmdLets, and Functions which are part of Powershell. I have done these in both 32bit and 64bit.

I have also included a 32bit and 64bit version of Windows Management Instrumentation (WMI) that will help you build command line calls.

Below is one of them:

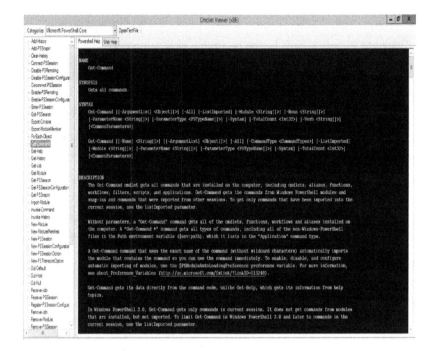

This one is in 64 bit:

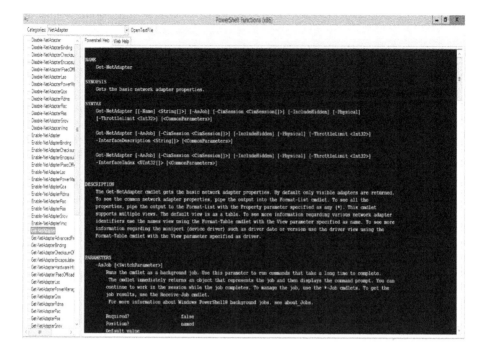

```
PowerShell Functions (x86)                                                    _ □ X

Categories: NetAdapter          ▼   OpenTextFile

Disable-NetAdapter          ^  Powershell Help  Web Help
Disable-NetAdapterBinding
Disable-NetAdapterChecksu       NAME
Disable-NetAdapterEncapsu          Get-NetAdapter
Disable-NetAdapterIPsecOffl
Disable-NetAdapterLso           SYNOPSIS
Disable-NetAdapterPowerMa          Gets the basic network adapter properties.
Disable-NetAdapterQos
Disable-NetAdapterRdma          SYNTAX
Disable-NetAdapterRsc              Get-NetAdapter [[-Name] <String[]>] [-AsJob] [-CimSession <CimSession[]>] [-IncludeHidden] [-Physical]
Disable-NetAdapterRss              [-ThrottleLimit <Int32>] [<CommonParameters>]
Disable-NetAdapterSriov
Disable-NetAdapterVmq              Get-NetAdapter [-AsJob] [-CimSession <CimSession[]>] [-IncludeHidden] [-Physical] [-ThrottleLimit <Int32>]
Enable-NetAdapter                  -InterfaceDescription <String[]> [<CommonParameters>]
Enable-NetAdapterBinding
Enable-NetAdapterChecksur          Get-NetAdapter [-AsJob] [-CimSession <CimSession[]>] [-IncludeHidden] [-Physical] [-ThrottleLimit <Int32>]
Enable-NetAdapterEncapsul          -InterfaceIndex <UInt32[]> [<CommonParameters>]
Enable-NetAdapterIPsecOffl
Enable-NetAdapterLso
Enable-NetAdapterPowerMa        DESCRIPTION
Enable-NetAdapterQos               The Get-NetAdapter cmdlet gets the basic network adapter properties. By default only visible adapters are returned.
Enable-NetAdapterRdma              To see the common network adapter properties, pipe the output into the Format-List cmdlet. To see all the
Enable-NetAdapterRsc               properties, pipe the output to the Format-List with the Property parameter specified as any (*). This cmdlet
Enable-NetAdapterRss               supports multiple views. The default view is as a table. To see more information regarding various network adapter
Enable-NetAdapterSriov             identifiers use the names view using the Format-Table cmdlet with the View parameter specified as name. To see more
Enable-NetAdapterVmq               information regarding the miniport (device driver) such as driver date or version use the driver view using the
Get-NetAdapter                     Format-Table cmdlet with the View parameter specified as driver.
Get-NetAdapterAdvancedPr
Get-NetAdapterBinding           PARAMETERS
Get-NetAdapterChecksumOf           -AsJob [<SwitchParameter>]
Get-NetAdapterEncapsulate             Runs the cmdlet as a background job. Use this parameter to run commands that take a long time to complete.
Get-NetAdapterHardwareInf          The cmdlet immediately returns an object that represents the job and then displays the command prompt. You can
Get-NetAdapterLso                  continue to work in the session while the job completes. To manage the job, use the *-Job cmdlets. To get the
Get-NetAdapterPowerManag           job results, use the Receive-Job cmdlet.
Get-NetAdapterQos                  For more information about Windows PowerShell® background jobs, see about_Jobs.
Get-NetAdapterRdma
Get-NetAdapterRss                     Required?              false
Get-NetAdapterSriov     v             Position?              named
<      III      >                     Default value
```

Learn by creating a problem and solving it.

THE PROBLEM:

Your boss says, "Need a script that Produces a connection in ADO, connects to Access recordset and spits out an HTML Report based on a particular table. Can you do it?

I know what I would be thinking, what the he double hockey sticks is wrong with him? Do I look like a programmer?

Well, of course, I am. So here's what I would be thinking. I'm about to fuel an addiction that will keep me around for another 6 months. So I say, "Sure, just tell me where the database is located and I can take it from there."

"How long will it take you?" he asks.

(Snicker, snicker). "About two days. One to write the script. Another test and make the changes you want"

He thinks for a moment, "Alright, here's the location of the file."

Normally, what appears to be a simple task like this becomes a week.

We're going to do it in 30 seconds.

But before we do, I have to cover these points:

1. You need to establish a crystal agreement between you and your boss. One, that the only thing he wants is a report and nothing else. If that is not agreed upon before you agree to move forward on this project, you could end up working on this on your off time and for free.
2. The core code that is necessary to do this task is less than 100 lines. Meaning if you spent the necessary time to write it, say 3 minutes per line, you vested time would be 5 hours. And that is .6 of an hour short of an entire day. Only if this project began at 9am the first day could you normally get it done in 2. So, you need to assure that the moment the agreement is made that it is based on 2 full days worth of work. Not now and tomorrow.
3. Any CSS or Cascading Stylesheet work to make the report visually stunning should not be part of the two days work. The one that is about to be used is 140 lines in itself.
4. Research time and the understanding of what coding will work to accomplish the task should also be agreed upon. Meaning a week of fulltime work on this project needed to be agreed to as well.

SOLUTION:

This is a standard stock solutions requiring:

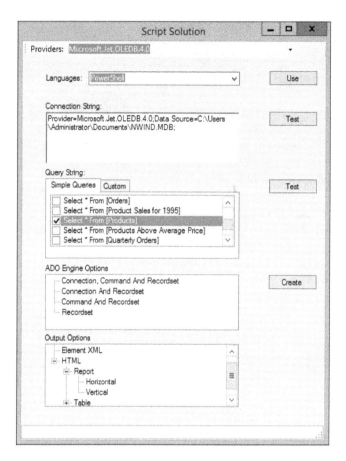

Okay, so since I already have a tool created, I start by running the x86 version to see if I can find a Provider to work with the boss' Access Database. Sure enough, there is and I use it to open it.

If this is successful, I then enumerate through the tables and populate my list of simply queries as shown above. I then have the option to decide what ADO components I want to use and polish off the selections with a HTML Report with a Horizontal orientation. Then I click create.

That produces this:

```
$cn = new-object -com ADODB.Connection
$cmd = new-object -com ADODB.Command
$rs = new-object -com ADODB.Recordset

$cn.ConnectionString = "Provider=Microsoft.Jet.OLEDB.4.0;Data
Source=C:\Users\Administrator\Documents\NWIND.MDB;"
$cn.Open()

$cmd.ActiveConnection = $cn
$cmd.CommandType = 1
$cmd.CommandText = "Select * From [Orders]"
$cmd.Execute()

$rs.LockType = 3
$rs.CursorLocation = 3
$rs.Open($cmd)

$ws = new-object -com WScript.Shell
$fso = new-object -com Scripting.FileSystemObject
$txtstream = $fso.OpenTextFile($ws.CurrentDirectory + "\NWIND.html", 2, $true, -2)
$txtstream.WriteLine("<html>")
$txtstream.WriteLine("<head>")
$txtstream.WriteLine("<title>NWIND</title>")
$txtstream.writeline("<style type='text/css'>")
$txtstream.writeline("body")
$txtstream.writeline("{")
$txtstream.writeline("PADDING-RIGHT: 0px;")
$txtstream.writeline("PADDING-LEFT: 0px;")
$txtstream.writeline("PADDING-BOTTOM: 0px;")
$txtstream.writeline("MARGIN: 0px;")
$txtstream.writeline("COLOR: #333;")
$txtstream.writeline("PADDING-TOP: 0px;")
$txtstream.writeline("FONT-FAMILY: verdana, arial, helvetica, sans-serif;")
$txtstream.writeline("}")
$txtstream.writeline("table")
$txtstream.writeline("{")
$txtstream.writeline("BORDER-RIGHT: #999999 3px solid;")
$txtstream.writeline("PADDING-RIGHT: 6px;")
$txtstream.writeline("PADDING-LEFT: 6px;")
$txtstream.writeline("FONT-WEIGHT: Bold;")
$txtstream.writeline("FONT-SIZE: 14px;")
$txtstream.writeline("PADDING-BOTTOM: 6px;")
$txtstream.writeline("COLOR: Peru;")
$txtstream.writeline("LINE-HEIGHT: 14px;")
$txtstream.writeline("PADDING-TOP: 6px;")
$txtstream.writeline("BORDER-BOTTOM: #999 1px solid;")
$txtstream.writeline("BACKGROUND-COLOR: #eeeeee;")
$txtstream.writeline("FONT-FAMILY: verdana, arial, helvetica, sans-serif;")
$txtstream.writeline("FONT-SIZE: 12px;")
$txtstream.writeline("}")
$txtstream.writeline("th")
$txtstream.writeline("{")
$txtstream.writeline("BORDER-RIGHT: #999999 3px solid;")
```

```
$txtstream.writeline("PADDING-RIGHT: 6px;")
$txtstream.writeline("PADDING-LEFT: 6px;")
$txtstream.writeline("FONT-WEIGHT: Bold;")
$txtstream.writeline("FONT-SIZE: 14px;")
$txtstream.writeline("PADDING-BOTTOM: 6px;")
$txtstream.writeline("COLOR: darkred;")
$txtstream.writeline("LINE-HEIGHT: 14px;")
$txtstream.writeline("PADDING-TOP: 6px;")
$txtstream.writeline("BORDER-BOTTOM: #999 1px solid;")
$txtstream.writeline("BACKGROUND-COLOR: #eeeeee;")
$txtstream.writeline("FONT-FAMILY:font-family:Cambria, serif;")
$txtstream.writeline("FONT-SIZE: 12px;")
$txtstream.writeline("text-align: left;")
$txtstream.writeline("white-Space: nowrap;")
$txtstream.writeline("}")
$txtstream.writeline(".th")
$txtstream.writeline("{")
$txtstream.writeline("BORDER-RIGHT: #999999 2px solid;")
$txtstream.writeline("PADDING-RIGHT: 6px;")
$txtstream.writeline("PADDING-LEFT: 6px;")
$txtstream.writeline("FONT-WEIGHT: Bold;")
$txtstream.writeline("PADDING-BOTTOM: 6px;")
$txtstream.writeline("COLOR: darkred;")
$txtstream.writeline("PADDING-TOP: 6px;")
$txtstream.writeline("BORDER-BOTTOM: #999 2px solid;")
$txtstream.writeline("BACKGROUND-COLOR: #eeeeee;")
$txtstream.writeline("FONT-FAMILY: font-family:Cambria, serif;")
$txtstream.writeline("FONT-SIZE: 10px;")
$txtstream.writeline("text-align: right;")
$txtstream.writeline("white-Space: nowrap;")
$txtstream.writeline("}")
$txtstream.writeline("td")
$txtstream.writeline("{")
$txtstream.writeline("BORDER-RIGHT: #999999 3px solid;")
$txtstream.writeline("PADDING-RIGHT: 6px;")
$txtstream.writeline("PADDING-LEFT: 6px;")
$txtstream.writeline("FONT-WEIGHT: Normal;")
$txtstream.writeline("PADDING-BOTTOM: 6px;")
$txtstream.writeline("COLOR: navy;")
$txtstream.writeline("LINE-HEIGHT: 14px;")
$txtstream.writeline("PADDING-TOP: 6px;")
$txtstream.writeline("BORDER-BOTTOM: #999 1px solid;")
$txtstream.writeline("BACKGROUND-COLOR: #eeeeee;")
$txtstream.writeline("FONT-FAMILY: font-family:Cambria, serif;")
$txtstream.writeline("FONT-SIZE: 12px;")
$txtstream.writeline("text-align: left;")
$txtstream.writeline("white-Space: nowrap;")
$txtstream.writeline("}")
$txtstream.writeline(".td")
$txtstream.writeline("{")
$txtstream.writeline("BORDER-RIGHT: #999999 3px solid;")
$txtstream.writeline("PADDING-RIGHT: 6px;")
$txtstream.writeline("PADDING-LEFT: 6px;")
```

```
$txtstream.writeline("FONT-WEIGHT: Normal;")
$txtstream.writeline("PADDING-BOTTOM: 6px;")
$txtstream.writeline("COLOR: black;")
$txtstream.writeline("PADDING-TOP: 6px;")
$txtstream.writeline("BORDER-BOTTOM: #999 1px solid;")
$txtstream.writeline("BACKGROUND-COLOR: navy;")
$txtstream.writeline("FONT-FAMILY: font-family:Cambria, serif;")
$txtstream.writeline("FONT-SIZE: 10px;")
$txtstream.writeline("text-align: left;")
$txtstream.writeline("white-Space: nowrap;")
$txtstream.writeline("}")
$txtstream.writeline("div")
$txtstream.writeline("{")
$txtstream.writeline("BORDER-RIGHT: #999999 3px solid;")
$txtstream.writeline("PADDING-RIGHT: 6px;")
$txtstream.writeline("PADDING-LEFT: 6px;")
$txtstream.writeline("FONT-WEIGHT: Normal;")
$txtstream.writeline("PADDING-BOTTOM: 6px;")
$txtstream.writeline("COLOR: white;")
$txtstream.writeline("PADDING-TOP: 6px;")
$txtstream.writeline("BORDER-BOTTOM: #999 1px solid;")
$txtstream.writeline("BACKGROUND-COLOR: navy;")
$txtstream.writeline("FONT-FAMILY: font-family:Cambria, serif;")
$txtstream.writeline("FONT-SIZE: 10px;")
$txtstream.writeline("text-align: left;")
$txtstream.writeline("white-Space: nowrap;")
$txtstream.writeline("}")
$txtstream.writeline("span")
$txtstream.writeline("{")
$txtstream.writeline("BORDER-RIGHT: #999999 3px solid;")
$txtstream.writeline("PADDING-RIGHT: 3px;")
$txtstream.writeline("PADDING-LEFT: 3px;")
$txtstream.writeline("FONT-WEIGHT: Normal;")
$txtstream.writeline("PADDING-BOTTOM: 3px;")
$txtstream.writeline("COLOR: white;")
$txtstream.writeline("PADDING-TOP: 3px;")
$txtstream.writeline("BORDER-BOTTOM: #999 1px solid;")
$txtstream.writeline("BACKGROUND-COLOR: navy;")
$txtstream.writeline("FONT-FAMILY: font-family:Cambria, serif;")
$txtstream.writeline("FONT-SIZE: 10px;")
$txtstream.writeline("text-align: left;")
$txtstream.writeline("white-Space: nowrap;")
$txtstream.writeline("display:inline-block;")
$txtstream.writeline("width: 100%;")
$txtstream.writeline("}")
$txtstream.writeline("textarea")
$txtstream.writeline("{")
$txtstream.writeline("BORDER-RIGHT: #999999 3px solid;")
$txtstream.writeline("PADDING-RIGHT: 3px;")
$txtstream.writeline("PADDING-LEFT: 3px;")
$txtstream.writeline("FONT-WEIGHT: Normal;")
$txtstream.writeline("PADDING-BOTTOM: 3px;")
$txtstream.writeline("COLOR: white;")
```

```
$txtstream.writeline("PADDING-TOP: 3px;")
$txtstream.writeline("BORDER-BOTTOM: #999 1px solid;")
$txtstream.writeline("BACKGROUND-COLOR: navy;")
$txtstream.writeline("FONT-FAMILY: font-family:Cambria, serif;")
$txtstream.writeline("FONT-SIZE: 10px;")
$txtstream.writeline("text-align: left;")
$txtstream.writeline("white-Space: nowrap;")
$txtstream.writeline("width: 100%;")
$txtstream.writeline("}")
$txtstream.writeline("select")
$txtstream.writeline("{")
$txtstream.writeline("BORDER-RIGHT: #999999 3px solid;")
$txtstream.writeline("PADDING-RIGHT: 6px;")
$txtstream.writeline("PADDING-LEFT: 6px;")
$txtstream.writeline("FONT-WEIGHT: Normal;")
$txtstream.writeline("PADDING-BOTTOM: 6px;")
$txtstream.writeline("COLOR: white;")
$txtstream.writeline("PADDING-TOP: 6px;")
$txtstream.writeline("BORDER-BOTTOM: #999 1px solid;")
$txtstream.writeline("BACKGROUND-COLOR: navy;")
$txtstream.writeline("FONT-FAMILY: font-family:Cambria, serif;")
$txtstream.writeline("FONT-SIZE: 10px;")
$txtstream.writeline("text-align: left;")
$txtstream.writeline("white-Space: nowrap;")
$txtstream.writeline("width: 100%;")
$txtstream.writeline("}")
$txtstream.writeline("input")
$txtstream.writeline("{")
$txtstream.writeline("BORDER-RIGHT: #999999 3px solid;")
$txtstream.writeline("PADDING-RIGHT: 3px;")
$txtstream.writeline("PADDING-LEFT: 3px;")
$txtstream.writeline("FONT-WEIGHT: Bold;")
$txtstream.writeline("PADDING-BOTTOM: 3px;")
$txtstream.writeline("COLOR: white;")
$txtstream.writeline("PADDING-TOP: 3px;")
$txtstream.writeline("BORDER-BOTTOM: #999 1px solid;")
$txtstream.writeline("BACKGROUND-COLOR: navy;")
$txtstream.writeline("FONT-FAMILY: font-family:Cambria, serif;")
$txtstream.writeline("FONT-SIZE: 12px;")
$txtstream.writeline("text-align: left;")
$txtstream.writeline("display:inline-block;")
$txtstream.writeline("white-Space: nowrap;")
$txtstream.writeline("}")
$txtstream.writeline("</style>")

$txtstream.WriteLine("</head>")
$txtstream.WriteLine("<body bgcolor=#333333>")
$txtstream.WriteLine("<center>")
$txtstream.WriteLine("<table colspacing=3 colpadding=3>")
$txtstream.WriteLine("<tr>")
for($x=0;$x -lt $rs.Fields.Count;$x++)
{
    $txtstream.WriteLine("<th>" + $rs.Fields[$x].Name  + "</th>")
```

```
    }
$txtstream.WriteLine("</tr>")

$rs.MoveLast()
$rs.MoveFirst()

while($rs.eof -eq $false)
{
    $txtstream.WriteLine("<tr>")
    for($x=0;$x -lt $rs.Fields.Count;$x++)
    {
        $txtstream.WriteLine("<td>" + $rs.Fields[$x].Value  + "</td>")
    }
    $txtstream.WriteLine("</tr>")
    $rs.MoveNext()
}
$txtstream.WriteLine("</table>")
$txtstream.WriteLine("</html>")
$txtstream.Close
```

That creates this and makes the boss happy for about 5 minutes.

Estimated time to write the same code out by hand with 231 lines at 2 minutes per line: 7.7 hours.

Time it took to start the program and create the script: 25 seconds.

Oh, wait, he doesn't want this in Powershell. He wants it in VBScript and it has to run on Server 2012R2 or higher.

THAT IS NOT GOING TO HAPPEN

Why? Because CScript and WScript -- the engines we use to run our scripts with are now 64 bit. And the program we are running and the scripts it is producing are 32bit.

Even if I run the program in 64bit mode

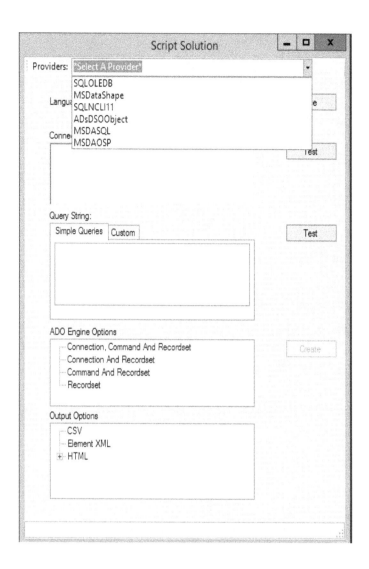

Wait a minute, I thought, isn't MSDAOSP a Element XML File Reader? Aren't we creating xml from our data engines in 32bit?

```
<?xml version='1.0' encoding='iso-8859-1'?>
<data>
<products>
<ProductID>1</ProductID>
<ProductName>Chai</ProductName>
<SupplierID>1</SupplierID>
<CategoryID>1</CategoryID>
```

```
<QuantityPerUnit>10 boxes x 20 bags</QuantityPerUnit>
<UnitPrice>18</UnitPrice>
<UnitsInStock>39</UnitsInStock>
<UnitsOnOrder>0</UnitsOnOrder>
<ReorderLevel>10</ReorderLevel>
<Discontinued>False</Discontinued>
</products>
<products>
<ProductID>2</ProductID>
<ProductName>Chang</ProductName>
<SupplierID>1</SupplierID>
<CategoryID>1</CategoryID>
<QuantityPerUnit>24 - 12 oz bottles</QuantityPerUnit>
<UnitPrice>19</UnitPrice>
<UnitsInStock>17</UnitsInStock>
<UnitsOnOrder>40</UnitsOnOrder>
<ReorderLevel>25</ReorderLevel>
<Discontinued>False</Discontinued>
</products>
```

So, why not put the data into xml where the 32bit engine could spit out the XML And the 64bit script could read it and produce a report from it?

Since all we need is a recordset,

```
Set cn = CreateObject("ADODB.Connection")
cn.Open ("Provider=MSDAOSP;Data Source=Msxml2.DSOControl")

Set rs = CreateObject("ADODB.Recordset")
rs.ActiveConnection = cn
rs.Open ("C:\products.xml")
```

After that, the rest of the code can use the Recordset logic and create the report.

Discontinued	$Text
False	1 Chai 1 1 10 boxes x 20 bags 18 39 0 10 False
False	2 Chang 1 1 24 - 12 oz bottles 19 17 40 25 False
False	3 Aniseed Syrup 1 2 12 - 550 ml bottles 10 13 70 25 False
False	4 Chef Anton's Cajun Seasoning 2 2 48 - 6 oz jars 22 53 0 0 False
True	5 Chef Anton's Gumbo Mix 2 2 36 boxes 21.35 0 0 0 True
False	6 Grandma's Boysenberry Spread 3 2 12 - 8 oz jars 25 120 0 25 False
False	7 Uncle Bob's Organic Dried Pears 3 7 12 - 1 lb pkgs. 30 15 0 10 False
False	8 Northwoods Cranberry Sauce 3 2 12 - 12 oz jars 40 6 0 0 False
True	9 Mishi Kobe Niku 4 6 18 - 500 g pkgs. 97 29 0 0 True
False	10 Ikura 4 8 12 - 200 ml jars 31 31 0 0 False
False	11 Queso Cabrales 5 4 1 kg pkg. 21 22 30 30 False
False	12 Queso Manchego La Pastora 5 4 10 - 500 g pkgs. 38 86 0 0 False
False	13 Konbu 6 8 2 kg box 6 24 0 5 False
False	14 Tofu 6 7 40 - 100 g pkgs. 23.25 35 0 0 False

I'm showing you the above image because when you work with XML, the MSDAOSP provider adds an additional field with a summary of all the text that row.

In-other-words, it worked.

```
Set cn = CreateObject("ADODB.Connection")
cn.Open ("Provider=MSDAOSP;Data Source=Msxml2.DSOControl")

Set rs = CreateObject("ADODB.Recordset")
rs.ActiveConnection = cn
rs.Open ("C:\products.xml")

Set ws = CreateObject("WScript.Shell")
$fso = new-object -com Scripting.FileSystemObject
Set txtstream = $fso.OpenTextFile(ws.CurrentDirectory & "\products.html", 2, True, -2)
txtstream.writeline("<html>")
txtstream.writeline("<head>")
txtstream.writeline("<title>products</title>")
txtstream.writeline("</head>")
txtstream.writeline("<body bgcolor=#333333>")
txtstream.writeline("<center>")
txtstream.writeline("<table colspacing=3 colpadding=3>")
```

```
    txtstream.writeline("<tr>")
    For x = 0 to rs.Fields.Count-2
        txtstream.writeline("<th>" & rs.Fields(x).Name & "</th>")
    Next
    txtstream.writeline("</tr>")

rs.MoveLast()
rs.MoveFirst()

    Do While not rs.eof
        txtstream.writeline("<tr>")
        For x = 0 to rs.Fields.Count-2
            txtstream.writeline("<td>" & rs.Fields(x).Value & "</td>")
        Next
        txtstream.writeline("</tr>")
    rs.MoveNext()
    Loop
    txtstream.writeline("</table>")
    txtstream.writeline("</html>")
    txtstream.Close
```

And the results without the last field:

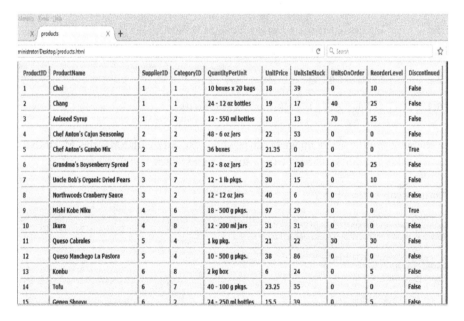

So, what was the point to all of this?

We just created a work around that enabled a 64bit program to communicate with a 32bit program's output.

This concept is better known as Customer Relationship Management or CRM for short.

I've created a lot of tools for you to work with. Since there is two versions of PowerShell, everything I have built comes in pairs.

Here's my 32bit version of my CmdLet reader:

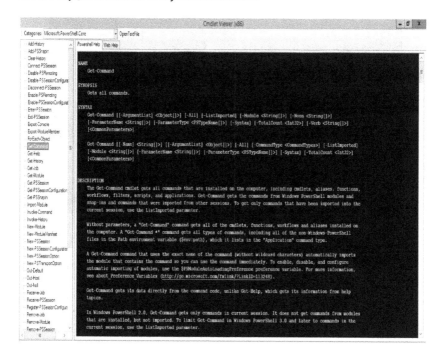

This one is in 64 bit:

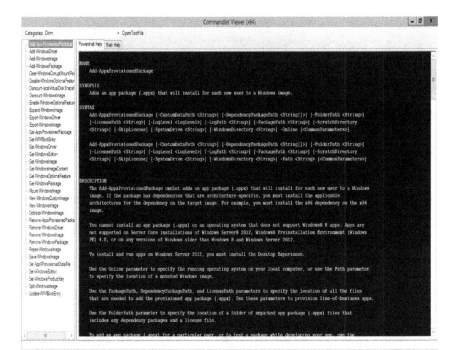

Commandlet Viewer (x64)

Categories: Dism   ▼ OpenTextFile

PowerShell Help | Web Help

Add-AppxProvisionedPackage
Add-WindowsDriver
Add-WindowsImage
Add-WindowsPackage
Clear-WindowsCorruptMountPoi
Disable-WindowsOptionalFeatur
Dismount-localVirtualDiskSnapsh
Dismount-WindowsImage
Enable-WindowsOptionalFeatur
Expand-WindowsImage
Export-WindowsDriver
Export-WindowsImage
Get-AppxProvisionedPackage
Get-WIMBootEntry
Get-WindowsDriver
Get-WindowsEdition
Get-WindowsImage
Get-WindowsImageContent
Get-WindowsOptionalFeature
Get-WindowsPackage
Mount-WindowsImage
New-WindowsCustomImage
New-WindowsImage
Optimize-WindowsImage
Remove-AppxProvisionedPacka
Remove-WindowsDriver
Remove-WindowsImage
Remove-WindowsPackage
Repair-WindowsImage
Save-WindowsImage
Set-AppxProvisionedDataFile
Set-WindowsEdition
Set-WindowsProductKey
Split-WindowsImage
Update-WIMBootEntry

NAME

    Add-AppxProvisionedPackage

SYNOPSIS

    Adds an app package (.appx) that will install for each new user to a Windows image.

SYNTAX

    Add-AppxProvisionedPackage [-CustomDataPath <String>] [-DependencyPackagePath <String[]>] [-FolderPath <String>]
    [-LicensePath <String>] [-LogLevel <LogLevel>] [-LogPath <String>] [-PackagePath <String>] [-ScratchDirectory
    <String>] [-SkipLicense] [-SystemDrive <String>] [-WindowsDirectory <String>] -Online [<CommonParameters>]

    Add-AppxProvisionedPackage [-CustomDataPath <String>] [-DependencyPackagePath <String[]>] [-FolderPath <String>]
    [-LicensePath <String>] [-LogLevel <LogLevel>] [-LogPath <String>] [-PackagePath <String>] [-ScratchDirectory
    <String>] [-SkipLicense] [-SystemDrive <String>] [-WindowsDirectory <String>] -Path <String> [<CommonParameters>]

DESCRIPTION

    The Add-AppxProvisionedPackage cmdlet adds an app package (.appx) that will install for each new user to a Windows
    image. If the package has dependencies that are architecture-specific, you must install the applicable
    architectures for the dependency on the target image. For example, you must install the x86 dependency on the x86
    image.

    You cannot install an app package (.appx) on an operating system that does not support Windows® 8 apps. Apps are
    not supported on Server Core installations of Windows Server® 2012, Windows® Preinstallation Environment (Windows
    PE) 4.0, or on any versions of Windows older than Windows 8 and Windows Server 2012.

    To install and run apps on Windows Server 2012, you must install the Desktop Experience.

    Use the Online parameter to specify the running operating system on your local computer, or use the Path parameter
    to specify the location of a mounted Windows image.

    Use the PackagePath, DependencyPackagePath, and LicensePath parameters to specify the location of all the files
    that are needed to add the provisioned app package (.appx). Use these parameters to provision line-of-business apps.

    Use the FolderPath parameter to specify the location of a folder of unpacked app package (.appx) files that
    includes any dependency packages and a license file.

    To add an app package (.appx) for a particular user, or to test a package while developing your app, use the

Programming 101

f you are wondering what programming is, according to most descriptions, this is the most agreed upon one:

Programming is the process of taking an algorithm and encoding it into a notation, a programming language, so that it can be executed by a computer. Although many programming languages and many different types of computers exist, the important first step is the need to have the solution. Without an algorithm there can be no program.

Unfortunately, I have no idea what that just said. ⊠

I think what this description is saying is that real programs are assembly, c, and c++ programmers who write the blood and guts stuff – JNE or Jump if not equal -- and the rest of us are high level programmers. Depending on them for our livelihood.

Of course, none of that helped me get my first job at Microsoft..

Below, is what got me my job at Microsoft. Remember, I said I learned programming by reading books and pulling out from them what interested me?

Reading and understanding existing code is how I landed my first job at Microsoft. In 1996, I started at a hourly wage of $35\hour.

All the symbols that I just covered above put these 12 lines of code into motion.

Below is an example of putting the 12 possible lines into action:

```
function Populate_The_Table()
```

```
{
        param
        (
        [object]$objs,
        [string]$Query
        )
        $rs1 = $db.OpenRecordset($Query)
        while($rs.eof -eq $false)
        {
                $rs1.Addnew()
                for($x=0;$x -lt $rs.Fields.Count;$x++)
                {
                        $rs1.Fields[$x].Value = $rs.Fields[$x].Value
                }
                $rs1.Update()
        }
}
```

But the code I was reading and learning wasn't written in PowerShell, it was written in Visual Basic. And to be quite frank with you, is much easier to read

```
Public function Populate_The_Table(ByVal objs as Object, ByVal strQuery as String)

        Rs1 = db.OpenRecordset(strQuery)

        Rs1.AddNew()

        While (rs.eof = false)

                For x = 0 To rs.Fields.Count-1

                        Rs1.Fields(x).Value = rs.Fields(x).Value

                Next

                Rs1.Update()

        Loop
```

End Function

It is perfect in every way.

 That is, it is perfectly wrong.

Here's the issues:

1. There is no rs.MoveNext()
2. The object objs is never used
3. The code implies that db is a global object and is being referenced here from somewhere else.
4. The enumeration of the two records assumes they are identical and match each other
5. The function should be called a Sub in VB since it doesn't return a value
6. There are no comments. So we cannot know where db is coming from

When you look at code that uses a Component Object Model or COM created object , that object has a Document Object Model or DOM. The DOM dictates how the code will be written.

Therefore, you're looking at the programmer's understanding of what was required of him or her to perform an assignment that requires the use of that object.

For example, if you create an Access Application, the DOM associated with it dictates how intention is confined and formed around the DOM's framework.

Put another way, okay, if you are going to use me – the DOM for the Access.Application – these are the steps you have to take to do this correctly.

Therefore, the steps to go from here to there are predictable, never veering and provable.

So are the questions interviewers ask.

I would love to show you an image here of it but it is easier to point you to a link:

https://msdn.microsoft.com/en-us/library/aa266932(v=vs.60).aspx

Or an even better one can be found here.

http://codevba.com/msaccess/dao_objectmodeldiagram.xhtml#.WYAQ5FFlDIU

The Interviewer:

What command in Powershell will get you the actual properties of the recordset?

Empty or Opened?

Opened.

Well, after you have populated the recordset object, type in the name of the recordset and press enter.

Names	Values
Properties	System.___ComObject
BOF	FALSE
Bookmark	{0, 57, 2, 0}
Bookmarkable	TRUE
DateCreated	9/13/1995 10:51
EOF	FALSE
Filter	
Index	
LastModified	
LastUpdated	9/16/1996 18:22
LockEdits	TRUE
Name	Products
NoMatch	FALSE
Sort	
Transactions	TRUE
Type	1
RecordCount	77
Updatable	TRUE

Restartable	FALSE
ValidationText	
ValidationRule	
CacheStart	
CacheSize	
PercentPosition	0
AbsolutePosition	
EditMode	0
ODBCFetchCount	
ODBCFetchDelay	
Parent	System.___ComObject
Fields	System.___ComObject
hStmt	
StillExecuting	
BatchSize	
BatchCollisionCount	
BatchCollisions	
Connection	
RecordStatus	
UpdateOptions	

And for the Fields?

Well, after you have populated the recordset object, type in the name of the recordset, with a . and the word fields after it and press enter.

Name	Value
Properties	System.___ComObject
CollatingOrder	1033
Type	4

Name	ProductID
Size	4
SourceField	ProductID
SourceTable	Products
Value	1
Attributes	49
OrdinalPosition	0
ValidationText	
ValidateOnSet	FALSE
ValidationRule	
DefaultValue	
Required	FALSE
AllowZeroLength	FALSE
DataUpdatable	TRUE
ForeignName	
CollectionIndex	0
OriginalValue	
VisibleValue	
FieldSize	

Other questions included:

What's the difference between TableDefs and QueryDefs?

As the names suggests, TableDefs is a collection of Tables and Views and their definitions.

What tables are used by Microsoft and are usually filtered out of table option lists?

The tables not normally viewed or touched are the MSys tables.

PS C:\Users\Administrator> $tb | select-object name

Categories
Customers
Employees
MSysACEs
MSysCmdbars
MSysIMEXColumns
MSysIMEXSpecs
MSysModules
MSysModules2
MSysObjects
MSysQueries
MSysRelationships
Order Details
Orders
Products
Shippers
Suppliers

What are QueryDefs?

QueryDefs are essentially, stored procedures.

```
PS C:\> $QD = $db.QueryDefs
PS C:\> $QD
```

```
Properties    : System.___ComObject
DateCreated   : 6/21/1996 6:18:30 PM
LastUpdated   : 9/23/1996 3:23:36 PM
Name          : Alphabetical List of Products
ODBCTimeout   : 0
Type          : 0
SQL           : SELECT DISTINCTROW Products.*, Categories.CategoryName
                        FROM Categories INNER JOIN Products ON Categories.CategoryID = Products.CategoryID
        WHERE (((Products.Discontinued)=No));
```

I was asked what's the difference between an Inner Join and an Outer Join.

I don't know. But if you show me, I'm willing to learn.

Really, that's what I said. Being dyslexic doesn't help when you are trying to learn logic.

I still don't know. No one has ever shown me.

This is, perhaps, the best answer.

And if asked, we filter out the "MSys" because these are system tables and we use []
around all tables in DAO because everyone else in the world uses solid names verses
user friendly names because the rest of the world doesn't use spaces between
tablenames.

If you know all above from page 17 to here, then you know what I had to know to
land a job at Microsoft.

Wait a minute, did you just say I could land a job now?

No, what I just covered landed me a job at Microsoft back in 1996. But the core
ingredients are the same for every job that interviews you.

1. You need to have a passion for the potential work you will be doing
2. You need to show a sincere enthusiasm and understanding of the business'
    goals and objectives
3. You need to be willing to show the interviewer\s what you know and
    explain it clearly
4. You need to be willing to say you don't know when you don't
5. You need to be willing to ask questions that voice interest in the job
6. You need to be willing to have fun with the interview.

Depends on the job requirements.

Yes, with what I just covered, you could land a job in technical support or as a
beginning PowerShell programmer.

It is this foot in the door that keeps you thirsty to learn more and more and more!

I have also learned that after three attempts at trying something new, finding it on
the way and trying it that way, well, if it works, it's a keeper.

I also spend lots of time tinkering around with "what if" possibilities. That's the
writer in me.

It is all about the DOM

O kay, so what, exactly, is the DOM?

DOM is yet another acronym for Document Object Model. It is the primary reason why when you code with an IDE that has something like Intellisense that it is able to help you write the code. This wasn't around when VB3 or VB4 came out. So you learned how to write your code through trial and error.

There isn't just one. In fact, technically speaking there should be a DOM for every object that gets created. I can tell you that even after .Net proved VB.Net was and still is the most powerful programming language on the planet, special interest groups would like you to believe that C# is the most popular – or when .Net wasn't around – C++ was.

So a lot of the functionality of very choice servings of crucial programs just happened to be missing DOMs and couldn't be used by VB programmers. And wouldn't you know, the majority of the coding examples are done in C# up on the MSDN.

Fact is, there is potentially one of these beast for almost every object you create in .Net. How is that possible? I'll show you in just a moment.

I look at DOMs as though they are a treasure map or, if you want to dispel with the Indiana Jones romance, roadmap that I had to learn to read to get the treasure chest or to my destination where knowledge and understanding come together and help me see the ways to make the code work when necessary to get to code complete.

How do you read a DOM? Well, that gets a bit complicated for a couple of reasons. Some DOMS are so popular that actual graphical charts have been created. Other s, because they are more COM and less .Net have none.

Technically speaking, they – COM and NET -- are supposed to be different enough that one or the other could be eliminated and the other would have the swagger to do get the same job done..

Truth is, COM is the underlying fabric .Net is sown into. Without COM, .Net would not exist.

So, you might think, based on this that there are no differences between how you would discover the information from a COM based object and a .Net based object.

And you would be correct.

Which is why, a lot of people want VB.Net to go away.

Because VB.Net makes it so darn easy to do both and make money with less effort.

Mirror, Mirror on the wall, whats the easiest way to the DOM of all

One single word: Reflection. (Hey, I thought I was being cute with the mirror thingy.)

Suppose I wanted to know what's under the hood when I create WScript.Shell. How would I do it in Powershell?

```
$ws = new-object -comobj WScript.Shell
$ws | get-member
```

This is the output:

```
PS C:\Users\Administrator> $ws = new-object -comobj WScript.Shell
PS C:\Users\Administrator> $ws | get-member


   TypeName: System.__ComObject#{41904400-be18-11d3-a28b-00104bd35090}

Name                     MemberType           Definition
----                     ----------           ----------
AppActivate              Method               bool AppActivate (Variant, Variant)
CreateShortcut           Method               IDispatch CreateShortcut (string)
Exec                     Method               IWshExec Exec (string)
ExpandEnvironmentStrings Method               string ExpandEnvironmentStrings (string)
LogEvent                 Method               bool LogEvent (Variant, string, string)
Popup                    Method               int Popup (string, Variant, Variant, Variant)
RegDelete                Method               void RegDelete (string)
RegRead                  Method               Variant RegRead (string)
RegWrite                 Method               void RegWrite (string, Variant, Variant)
Run                      Method               int Run (string, Variant, Variant)
SendKeys                 Method               void SendKeys (string, Variant)
Environment              ParameterizedProperty IWshEnvironment Environment (Variant) {get}
CurrentDirectory         Property             string CurrentDirectory () {get} {set}
SpecialFolders           Property             IWshCollection SpecialFolders () {get}
```

Only problem is, that only works in Powershell!

If I do the same in VB.Net:

```
Dim ws As Object = CreateObject("WScript.Shell")
Dim t As Type = ws.GetType
Debug.Print(t.Name)
Dim tempstr As String = ""
For Each mem As MemberInfo In t.GetMembers
    If mem.MemberType = MemberTypes.Event Then
        tempstr = "Event"
    End If
    If mem.MemberType = MemberTypes.Method Then
        tempstr = "Event"
    End If
    If mem.MemberType = MemberTypes.Property Then
        tempstr = "Property"
    End If
    Debug.Print(mem.Name.PadRight(30) & tempstr.PadRight(15, " ") & mem.ToString())
Next
```

It returns this:

```
___ComObject

ToString            Event   System.String ToString()
GetLifetimeService       Event   System.Object GetLifetimeService()
```

49

```
InitializeLifetimeService    Event    System.Object InitializeLifetimeService()
CreateObjRef                 Event    System.Runtime.Remoting.ObjRef CreateObjRef(System.Type)
Equals               Event    Boolean Equals(System.Object)
GetHashCode                  Event    Int32 GetHashCode()
GetType              Event    System.Type GetType()
```

These are the COM interfaces and not the actual information that you see when you run the same thing in Powershell. So, how does Powershell get away with it and you can't?

When you type –com, you are telling PowerShell to switch from reflection to TLI or the COM version of reflection..

Now, let's go see what we can do typelibInfo.

So, we start off with this:

```
Dim tfo As TLI.InterfaceInfo
Dim tliapp As New TLIApplication
Dim obj As Object = CreateObject("WScript.Shell")
tfo = tliapp.InterfaceInfoFromObject(obj)
Debug.Print(tfo.Name)
For Each mem As TLI.MemberInfo In tfo.Members
   Debug.Print(mem.Name)
Next
```

And it returns with this.

```
                   IWshShell3

                   Exec
                   CurrentDirectory
                   CurrentDirectory
```

Basically, its saying I have a method called Exec and a property called CurrentDirectory that can be read and written.

While I don't know why it is doing this, I do know how to fix it.

```
Dim cfo As CoClassInfo
Dim tfo As TLI.InterfaceInfo
Dim tliapp As New TLIApplication
Dim obj As Object = CreateObject("WScript.Shell")
tfo = tliapp.InterfaceInfoFromObject(obj)
For Each cfo In tfo.Parent.CoClasses
   For Each tfo In cfo.Interfaces

      If tfo.Name = "IWshShell3" Then

         For Each mem As TLI.MemberInfo In tfo.Members
```

```
            Select Case mem.Name

                    Case "QueryInterface", "AddRef", "Release", "GetTypeInfoCount", "GetTypeInfo",
"GetIDsOfNames", "Invoke"

                Case Else

                    Debug.Print(mem.Name)

            End Select

        Next

        Exit Sub

    End If

    Next

    Next
```

Okay, so., what is going on with this code? Well, since I know what Interface I want, I'm back up into the TLI DOM to the Parent.CoClasses level.

I also know, based on years worth of experience working with TypeLibInfo, that all classes will have at least one interface of the same name and possibly a second to support events.

Anyway, I cleaned up the output – getting rid of the COM related members and it left me with this:

```
Class: WshShell
Interface: IWshShell3

Members:
SpecialFolders
Environment
Run
Popup
CreateShortcut
ExpandEnvironmentStrings
RegRead
RegWrite
RegDelete
LogEvent
AppActivate
SendKeys
```

```
PS C:\Users\Administrator> $ws = new-object -comobj WScript.Shell
PS C:\Users\Administrator> $ws | get-member


    TypeName: System.__ComObject#{41904400-be18-11d3-a28b-00104bd35090}

Name                      MemberType            Definition
----                      ----------            ----------
AppActivate               Method                bool AppActivate (Variant, Variant)
CreateShortcut            Method                IDispatch CreateShortcut (string)
Exec                      Method                IWshExec Exec (string)
ExpandEnvironmentStrings  Method                string ExpandEnvironmentStrings (string)
LogEvent                  Method                bool LogEvent (Variant, string, string)
Popup                     Method                int Popup (string, Variant, Variant, Variant)
RegDelete                 Method                void RegDelete (string)
RegRead                   Method                Variant RegRead (string)
RegWrite                  Method                void RegWrite (string, Variant, Variant)
Run                       Method                int Run (string, Variant, Variant)
SendKeys                  Method                void SendKeys (string, Variant)
Environment               ParameterizedProperty IWshEnvironment Environment (Variant) {get}
CurrentDirectory          Property              string CurrentDirectory () {get} {set}
SpecialFolders            Property              IWshCollection SpecialFolders () {get}
```

Okay, so we have the members and from there, we can write the rest of the code to do the same thing Powershell did.

But do it with reflection?

```
Dim mystr As String
Dim obj As Object = CreateObject("WScript.Shell")
Dim t As System.Type = obj.GetType()
Dim i As Object = t.GetType().InvokeMember("IWshShell3", System.Reflection.BindingFlags.InvokeMethod, Nothing, t, Nothing)
For Each mem As System.Reflection.MemberInfo In i.Members

    Select Case mem.MemberType
```

> ⚠ MissingMethodException was unhandled
>
> Method 'System.RuntimeType.IWshShell3' not found.

That pretty much covers that.

WScript.Shell Explained

This particular object is probably one of the most powerful one. Especially for us. For a wide variety of reasons.

1. The $ws.CurrentDirectory is used in almost all of the examples.
2. Getting a list of Special Folders will help us later on
3. SendKeys can automate workflows
4. Run will be used to start Access and Excel and pull in a CSV text file
5. Popup will also be used later
6. CreateShortCut is a great way to place files on a user's desktop

That is 6 of 14 we're going to be using in this book.

With that said, let's dive into the deep end.

AppActivate

Best way to describe this one is it is a cool kind of weird.

```
PS C:\Users\Administrator> $ws.appActivate("Microsoft Access")
False
PS C:\Users\Administrator> $ws = new-object -com WScript.Shell
PS C:\Users\Administrator> $ws.Run("MSAccess")
0
PS C:\Users\Administrator> $ws.appActivate("Microsoft Access")
True
```

Okay, so what's happening here? Well, first off, AppActivate assumes that everything it should find is based on the parent: PowerShell's console window existence. So, if you already have an Access Application up before doing this, they don't exist.

So, even if you have MSAccess running, it won't see it. It will return false no matter what.

Now, we create an instance of Access by running the $ws.RunCommand:

```
$ws.Run("MSAccess")
```

And that brings up a new instance of Access.

So, you go back to PowerShell and type:

```
$ws.appActivate("Microsoft Access")
```

Access is again, the window commanding our attention. In-other-words, the method works to bring the window to the forefront.

CreateShortCut

Looks devilishly simple. $ws.CreateShortcut()

```
$nl = $ws.CreateShortcut("C:\users\Administrator\Desktop\VisualBasic.LNK")
$nl.TargetPath = "C:\Program Files (x86)\Microsoft Visual Studio\VB98\vb6.exe"
$nl.Arguments = ""
$nl.Description = "Visual Basic 6"
$nl.HotKey = "ALT+CTRL+F"
$nl.IconLocation = "C:\Program Files (x86)\Microsoft Visual Studio\VB98\vb6.exe "
$nl.WindowStyle = "1"
$nl.WorkingDirectory = "C:\Program Files (x86)\Microsoft Visual Studio\VB98"
$nl.Save()

$nl = $null
```

My link is now on my desktop.

EXEC

Works almost exactly like the Run version.

```
$ws = new-object –com WScript.Shell
$ws.exec("Calc")
```

ExpandEnvironmentSettings

```
$ws = new-object –com WScript.Shell
$fullpath = $ws.ExpandEnvironmentStrings("%windir%\notepad.exe, 0")
$ws.Popup ($fullpath)
```

LogEvent

This one is really fun!

Eventlog severity levels are the following:

```
 0  SUCCESS
 1  ERROR
 2  WARNING
 4  INFORMATION
 8  AUDIT_SUCCESS
16  AUDIT_FAILURE
```

```
$ws = new-object –com WScript.Shell
$ws.LogEvent(4, "You started reading this book!")
```

These events get recorded in the Application Log and look like this:

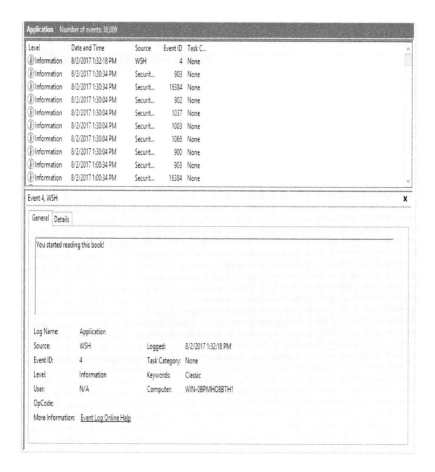

Believe me when I tell you this. You'll be back!

Popup

Just another way to let your users know something has happened.

```
$ws = new-object –com WScript.Shell
$ws.Popup( "You struck gold")
```

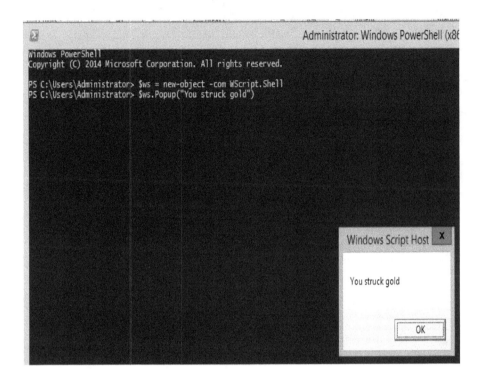

RegDelete, RegRead, RegWrite

I am not going to show you RegDelete or RegWrite. If you want to learn how to use those two, please feel free to do it on your own.

As for RegRead:

```
[string]$key = "HKEY_CLASSES_ROOT\MDACVer.Version\CurVer\"
$ws = new-object –com WScript.Shell
$ws.RegRead($key)
```

This returned:

MDACVer.Version.6.0

Run

Works almost exactly like the exec version.

```
$ws = new-object –com WScript.Shell
$ws.Run("Calc")
```

Sendkeys

Sendkeys is about the most cantankerous method that you will want to use. First, the program where you want to send the keys to has to be running and the active window. If you decide to use hot keys, the other program needs to be able to use them.

```
$ws = new-object –com WScript.Shell
$ws.Run("Excel")
[System.Threading.Thread]::Sleep(500)
$ws.SendKeys("Why did you wait this long to send me?")
```

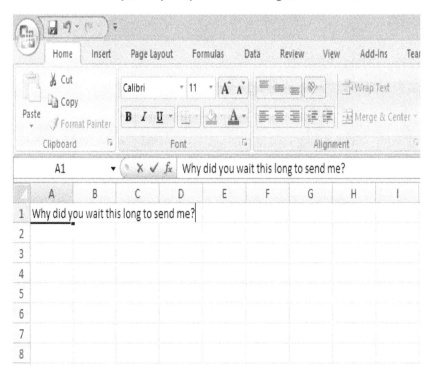

```
$ws = new-object –com WScript.Shell
$ws.Run("Notepad")
[System.Threading.Thread]::Sleep(500)
$ws.SendKeys("Wait, you forgot me!")
```

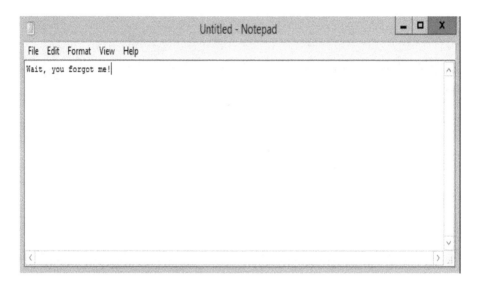

CurrentDirectory

You would be surprised to know just how many people don't know the Current Directory works both ways. You can get and set it as shown below:

```
PS C:\Users\Administrator> $cd = $ws.CurrentDirectory
PS C:\Users\Administrator> $cd
C:\Users\Administrator
PS C:\Users\Administrator> $cd = "C:\Users\Administrator\Desktop"
PS C:\Users\Administrator> $cd
C:\Users\Administrator\Desktop
```

Special Folders

Ever wonder what are special folders and how do you get to them? Neither did I ⊠ The code below will reveal them to you.

```
$ws = new-object -com WScript.Shell
$sf = $ws.SpecialFolders
$sf
```

Below is what PowerShell returns:

```
C:\Users\Public\Desktop
C:\ProgramData\Microsoft\Windows\Start Menu
C:\ProgramData\Microsoft\Windows\Start Menu\Programs
C:\ProgramData\Microsoft\Windows\Start Menu\Programs\StartUp
C:\Users\Administrator\Desktop
C:\Users\Administrator\AppData\Roaming
C:\Users\Administrator\AppData\Roaming\Microsoft\Windows\Printer
Shortcuts
C:\Users\Administrator\AppData\Roaming\Microsoft\Windows\Templates
C:\Windows\Fonts
C:\Users\Administrator\AppData\Roaming\Microsoft\Windows\Network
Shortcuts
C:\Users\Administrator\Desktop
C:\Users\Administrator\AppData\Roaming\Microsoft\Windows\Start Menu
C:\Users\Administrator\AppData\Roaming\Microsoft\Windows\SendTo
C:\Users\Administrator\AppData\Roaming\Microsoft\Windows\Recent
C:\Users\Administrator\AppData\Roaming\Microsoft\Windows\Start
Menu\Programs\Startup
C:\Users\Administrator\Favorites
C:\Users\Administrator\Documents
C:\Users\Administrator\AppData\Roaming\Microsoft\Windows\Start
Menu\Programs
```

Now that we've gone through all of what WScript.Shell object model has to offer, it is time to take your job expertise to the next level.

Since the coding for various Objects is defined and dictated by the object itself, there's little room for creativity and flexibility.

Working with WScript Network

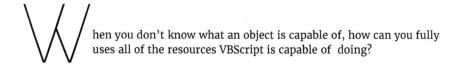hen you don't know what an object is capable of, how can you fully uses all of the resources VBScript is capable of doing?

Obviously, you can't. So, when I find something I think you're going to want to use, I'm going to show you things like the below table and then, I'm going to show you how to use them.

Name	MemberType	Definition
AddPrinterConnection	**Method**	void AddPrinterConnection (string, string, Variant, Variant, Variant)
AddWindowsPrinterConnection	**Method**	void AddWindowsPrinterConnection (string, string, string)
EnumNetworkDrives	**Method**	IWshCollection EnumNetworkDrives ()
EnumPrinterConnections	**Method**	IWshCollection EnumPrinterConnections ()
MapNetworkDrive	**Method**	MapNetworkDrive (string, string, Variant, Variant, Variant)

RemoveNetworkDrive	**Method**	void RemoveNetworkDrive (string, Variant, Variant)
RemovePrinterConnection	**Method**	void RemovePrinterConnection (string, Variant, Variant)
SetDefaultPrinter	**Method**	void SetDefaultPrinter (string)
ComputerName	**Property**	string ComputerName () {get}
Organization	**Property**	string Organization () {get}
Site	**Property**	string Site () {get}
UserDomain	**Property**	string UserDomain () {get}
UserName	**Property**	string UserName () {get}
UserProfile	**Property**	string UserProfile () {get}

Since I really am not interested - at this moment - with trying out the methods, what does work for us when I get the information by calling on each property with a {get} or a return value.

What's my computer Name

Open Notepad.
Type this in:

$wn = new-object -com WScript.Network
Write-host $wn.ComputerName
Save the file with Quotes around I as "ComputerName.ps1" And Double Click on it.
A window will popup telling you the Computer Name.

What's My Organization

Open Notepad.
Type this in:
$wn = new-object -com WScript.Network
Write-host $wn.Organization

Save the file with Quotes around I as "Organization.ps1"
Once the file is created, double click on it. A window will popup telling you the organization your computer belongs to.

WHAT'S THE NAME Of MY SITE

Open Notepad.
Type this in:

```
$wn = new-object -com WScript.Network
Write-host $wn.Site
```

Save the file with Quotes around I as "Site.ps1"
Once the file is created, double click on it. A window will popup telling you the name of your site.

WHAT'S MY USERDOMAIN

Open Notepad.
Type this in:

```
$wn = new-object -com WScript.Network
Write-host $wn.UserDomain
```

Save the file with Quotes around I as "Domain.ps1"
Once the file is created, double click on it. A window will popup telling you the Domain.

WHAT'S MY USERNAME

Open Notepad.
Type this in:

```
$wn = new-object -com WScript.Network
Write-host $wn.UserName
```

Save the file with Quotes around I as "UserName.ps1
Once the file is created, double click on it. A window will popup displaying your name.

WHAT'S MY USERPROFILE

Open Notepad.
Type this in:

```
$wn = new-object -com WScript.Network
Write-host $wn.UserProfile
```

Save the file with Quotes around I as "UserProfile.ps1"
Once the file is created, double click on it. A window will popup displaying your name.

THE MANY WAYS YOU CAN SAY HELLO

Open Notepad and type this:
```
'Just another way to let your users know something has happened.
$ws = new-object -com WScript.Shell
Write-host "Hello world"
$ws.Popup("Hello World!")
echo "Hello World"
```

Save the file as "HelloWorld.ps1". Once the file is created, double click on it. A window will popup telling you.

Working with the scripting object

t isn't built in but it should be. Scripting Object is a suite of tools which helps you to perform tasks that involve Drives, Folders, Files and creating and writing information out to files.

```
Name                  MemberType  Definition
----                  ----------  ----------
BuildPath             Method      string BuildPath (string, string)
CopyFile              Method      void CopyFile (string, string, bool)
CopyFolder            Method      void CopyFolder (string, string, bool)
CreateFolder          Method      IFolder CreateFolder (string)
CreateTextFile        Method      ITextStream CreateTextFile (string,
bool, bool)
DeleteFile            Method      void DeleteFile (string, bool)
DeleteFolder          Method      void DeleteFolder (string, bool)
DriveExists           Method      bool DriveExists (string)
FileExists            Method      bool FileExists (string)
FolderExists          Method      bool FolderExists (string)
GetAbsolutePathName   Method      string GetAbsolutePathName (string)
GetBaseName           Method      string GetBaseName (string)
GetDrive              Method      IDrive GetDrive (string)
GetDriveName          Method      string GetDriveName (string)
GetExtensionName      Method      string GetExtensionName (string)
GetFile               Method      IFile GetFile (string)
GetFileName           Method      string GetFileName (string)
GetFileVersion        Method      string GetFileVersion (string)
GetFolder             Method      IFolder GetFolder (string)
GetParentFolderName   Method      string GetParentFolderName (string)
```

```
GetSpecialFolder      Method      IFolder GetSpecialFolder
(SpecialFolderConst)
GetStandardStream     Method      ITextStream GetStandardStream
(StandardStreamTypes, bool)
GetTempName           Method      string GetTempName ()
MoveFile              Method      void MoveFile (string, string)
MoveFolder            Method      void MoveFolder (string, string)
OpenTextFile          Method      ITextStream OpenTextFile (string,
IOMode, bool, Tristate)
Drives                Property    IDriveCollection Drives () {get}
```

Let's take a look at each one.

BuildPath

The Build Path Function Returns a path and name combination. Below is an example of how it is used:

$Name = "Microsoft"
$fso = new-object -com Scripting.FileSystemObject

$bp = $fso.BuildPath("D:\", Name)
Write-host $bp

Note: This doesn't create the actual folder, it simply shows you how the path should look.

CopyFile

The CopyFile Function Copies a File from one location to another. Below is an example of how it is used:

$Source = "C:\Users\Administrator\Destkop\bMatch.vbs"
$Destination = "D:\Homeland\"
$fso = new-object -com Scripting.FileSystemObject
$iret = $fso.CopyFile($Source, $Destination, 1)

CopyFolder

The CopyFolder Function Copies a Folder from one location to another. Below is an example of how it is used:

```
$Source = "C:\Homeland"
$Destination = "D:\Users\Administrator\Desktop"
$fso = new-object -com Scripting.FileSystemObject
bp = $fso.CopyFolder($Source, $Destination, 1)
```

CreateFolder

The CreateFolder Function creates a Folder from a known path. Below is an example of how it is used:

```
$fso = new-object -com Scripting.FileSystemObject
$iret = $fso.CreateFolder("C:\Users\Administrator\Desktop\HopeChest")
```

CreateTextFile

The CreateTextFile function creates a text file in a known folder. Below is how it works:

```
$fso = new-object -com Scripting.FileSystemObject
$iret = $fso.CreateTextFile("C:\Users\Administrator\Desktop\HopeChest\Warren.txt", 1)
```

DeleteFile

The CreateTextFile function creates a text file in a known folder. Below is how it works:

```
$fso = new-object -com Scripting.FileSystemObject
$iret = $fso.DeleteFile("C:\Users\Administrator\Desktop\HopeChest\Warren.txt", 1)
```

DeleteFolder

The DeleteFolder Function deletes a folder and contents from a known path. Below is an example of how it is used:

Dim fso

$fso = new-object -com Scripting.FileSystemObject
$iret = $fso.DeleteFolder("C:\Users\Administrator\Desktop\Homeland")

DriveExists

Used to determine if a drive exists. Below is an example of it in use:

```
$fso = new-object -com Scripting.FileSystemObject

if ($fso.DriveExists("z") -eq $true)
{
   Write-host  "This drive exists"
}
else
{
   Write-host "This drive does not exist"
}
```

FileExists

Used to determine if a file exists. Below is an example of it in use:

$fso = new-object -com Scripting.FileSystemObject

   If($fso.FileExists("C:\Users\Administrator\Desktop\bMatch.vbs") -eq $true)

```
{
    Write-host  "This file exists"
}
else
{
    Write-host  "This file does not exist"
}
```

FolderExists

Used to determine if a folder exists. Below is an example of it in use:

```
$fso = new-object -com Scripting.FileSystemObjecti
if($fso.FolderExists("C:\Users\Administrator\Desktop\Homeland") -eq $true)
{
    Write-host ("This folder exists")
}
else
{
    Write-host ("This folder does not exist")
}
```

GetAbsolutePathName

GetAbsolutePathName is used to find out where the script is running. Below is an example of it in use:

```
$fso = new-object -com Scripting.FileSystemObject
$apn = $fso.GetAbsolutePathName("c:")
Write-host $apn
```

GetBaseName

GetBaseName is used to return just the name of the file. Below is an example of it in use:

```
$fso = new-object -com Scripting.FileSystemObject
$bn = $fso.GetBaseName("c:\Users\Administrator\Desktop\bMatch.vbs")
write-host $bn
```

GetDrive

GetDrive is used to reference a Drive and use that to enumerate folders and files on that drive. Below is an example of it in use:

```
$fso = new-object -com Scripting.FileSystemObject
$dr = $fso.GetDrive("c:\")
Foreach($fldr In $dr.RootFolder.SubFolders)
{
    write-host $fldr.Name
}
```

GetDriveName

GetDriveName is used to get the name from a specified file path. Below is an example of it in use:

```
$fso = new-object -com Scripting.FileSystemObject
$dn = $fso.GetDriveName("c:\users\Administrator\Desktop\bMatch.vbs")
write-host $dn
```

GetExtensionName

GetExtensionName is used to get the name of the extension from a specified file path. Below is an example of it in use:

```
$fso = new-object -com Scripting.FileSystemObject
$et = $fso.GetExtensionName("c:\users\Administrator\Desktop\bMatch.vbs")
write-host $et
```

GetFile

GetFile is used to get a reference a file that exists and display its properties. Below is an example of it in use:
Dim fso
Dim bp
Dim fldr

```
$fso = new-object -com Scripting.FileSystemObject
$dr = $fso.GetFile("c:\")
Foreach($fldr In $dr.RootFolder.SubFolders)
{
   Write-host  $fldr.Name
}
```

GetFileName

GetFileName function returns the name of a specified file. Below, is an example of it in use:

```
$fso = new-object -com Scripting.FileSystemObject
$fn = $fso.GetFileName("c:\users\Administrator\Desktop\bMatch.vbs")
Write-host  $fn
```

GetFileVersion

The GetFileVersion returns the version of a specified file. Below, is an example of it in use:

```
$fso = new-object -com Scripting.FileSystemObject
$fv = $fso.GetFileVersion("c:\users\Administrator\Desktop\bMatch.vbs")
Write-host  $fv
```

GetFolder

GetFolder is used to reference a folder and can be used to enumerate sub-folders and files in that folder. Below is an example of it in use:

```
$fso = new-object -com Scripting.FileSystemObject
$dr = $fso.GetFolder("c:\")
```

```
foreach($fldr In $dr.RootFolder.SubFolders)
{
   Write-host  $fldr.Name
}
```

GetParentFolderName

The GetParentFolderName function returns the parent folder. Below is an example of
is use:

```
$fso = new-object -com Scripting.FileSystemObject
$fn = $fso.GetParentFolderNamer("c:\Program Files")
Foreach($fldr In $dn.RootFolder.SubFolders)

{
   Write-host  $fldr.Name
}
```

GetSpecialFolder

This function can tell you what the Windows, System or temporary folder name is.
Below is an example of its use:

```
$fso = new-object -com Scripting.FileSystemObject
```

```
Windows:
$spf = $fso.GetSpecialFolder(0)
```

```
System:
$spf = $fso.GetSpecialFolder(1)
```

```
Temp:
$spf = $fso.GetSpecialFolder(2)
```

GetTempName

GetTempName is a function that returns a temporary name that can then be used as a way to create a file. Below is an example of it being used:

```
$fso = new-object -com Scripting.FileSystemObject
$temp = $fso.GetTempName()
```

MoveFile

The MoveFile Function moves a file from a known path to another known path. Below is an example of how it is used:

```
$source
$destination

$fso = new-object -com Scripting.FileSystemObject
$mf = $fso.MoveFile($Source, $Destination, $true)
```

MoveFolder

The MoveFolder Function moves a Folder from a known path to another known path. Below is an example of how it is used:

```
$source
$destination

$fso = new-object -com Scripting.FileSystemObject
$mf = $fso.MoveFolder($Source, $Destination)
```

OpenTextFile

OpenTextFile is used to read, write and append a text file. Below is an example of it in use:

For reading:

```
$fso = new-object -com Scripting.FileSystemObject
$txtstream = $fso.OpenTextFile("c:\Uses\Administrator\Desktop\myfile.txt", 1,
$false, -2)
```

For writing:

```
$fso = new-object -com Scripting.FileSystemObject
$txtstream = $fso.OpenTextFile("c:\Uses\Administrator\Desktop\myfile.txt", 2,
$true, -2)
```

For appending:

```
$fso = new-object -com Scripting.FileSystemObject
$txtstream = $fso.OpenTextFile("c:\Uses\Administrator\Desktop\myfile.txt", 8,
$true, -2)
```

Let's have some fun

I want to end this beginning book with a fun project and supply you with some stylesheets you can try with the output. Wouldn't you like to know some interesting stuff about your computer?

Okay, so here goes. The following are classes. Names of parts of your computer that you can call, create a webpage with and apply the CSS3 spreadsheets to.

Win32_BIOS
Win32_ComputerSystem
Win32_OperatingSystem
Win32_NetworkAdapter
Win32_NetworkLoginProfile
Win32_Process
Win32_Processor
Win32_Product
Win32_Service

You can plug these into the code below – one at a time, of course.

```
function GetValue{

    Param(
    [parameter(position=0)]
    $Name,
    [parameter(position=1)]
    $obj

    )
[string]$PName = $Name + " = "
$tempstr = $obj.GetObjectText_(0)
$pos = $tempstr.IndexOf($PName)
if ($pos -gt 0)
```

```powershell
    {
      $pos = $pos + $PName.Length
      $tempstr = $tempstr.SubString($pos, ($tempstr.Length - $pos))
      $pos = $tempstr.IndexOf(";")
      $tempstr = $tempstr.SubString(0, $pos)
      $tempstr = $tempstr.Replace("""", "")
      $tempstr = $tempstr.Replace("}", "")
      $tempstr = $tempstr.Replace("{", "")
      $tempstr = $tempstr.Trim()
      if($tempstr.Length -gt 14)
      {
        if($obj.Properties_.Item($Name).CIMType -eq 101)
        {
          [System.String]$tstr = $tempstr.SubString(4, 2)
          $tstr = $tstr + "/"
          $tstr = $tstr + $tempstr.SubString(6, 2)
          $tstr = $tstr + "/"
          $tstr = $tstr + $tempstr.SubString(0, 4)
          $tstr = $tstr + " "
          $tstr = $tstr + $tempstr.SubString(8, 2)
          $tstr = $tstr + ":"
          $tstr = $tstr + $tempstr.SubString(10, 2)
          $tstr = $tstr + ":"
          $tstr = $tstr + $tempstr.SubString(12, 2)
          $tempstr = $tstr
        }
      }
      return $tempstr
    }
    else
    {
      return ""
    }
}

$l = New-object -com WbemScripting.SWbemLocator
$svc = $l.ConnectServer(".", "root\cimv2")
$svc.Security_.AuthenticationLevel=6
$svc.Security_.ImpersonationLevel=3
$ob = $svc.Get("Win32_Process")
$objs = $ob.Instances_(0)
$ws = New-object -com WScript.Shell
$fso = New-object -com Scripting.FileSystemObject
$txtstream = $fso.OpenTextFile($ws.CurrentDirectory + "\\Win32_Process.html", 2,
$true, -2)
$txtstream.WriteLine("<html>")
$txtstream.WriteLine("<head>")
$txtstream.WriteLine("<style type='text/css'>")
$txtstream.WriteLine("th")
$txtstream.WriteLine("{")
```

```
$txtstream.WriteLine("    COLOR: darkred;")
$txtstream.WriteLine("    BACKGROUND-COLOR: white;")
$txtstream.WriteLine("    FONT-FAMILY:font-family: Cambria, serif;")
$txtstream.WriteLine("    FONT-SIZE: 12px;")
$txtstream.WriteLine("    text-align: left;")
$txtstream.WriteLine("    white-Space: nowrap;")
$txtstream.WriteLine("}")
$txtstream.WriteLine("td")
$txtstream.WriteLine("{")
$txtstream.WriteLine("    COLOR: navy;")
$txtstream.WriteLine("    BACKGROUND-COLOR: white;")
$txtstream.WriteLine("    FONT-FAMILY: font-family: Cambria, serif;")
$txtstream.WriteLine("    FONT-SIZE: 12px;")
$txtstream.WriteLine("    text-align: left;")
$txtstream.WriteLine("    white-Space: nowrap;")
$txtstream.WriteLine("}")
$txtstream.WriteLine("</style>")
$txtstream.WriteLine("<title>Win32_Process</title>")
$txtstream.WriteLine("</head>")
$txtstream.WriteLine("<body>")
#Use this if you want to create a border around your table:
#$txtstream.WriteLine("<table Border='1' cellpadding='1' cellspacing='1'>")
#Use this if you don't want to create a border around your table:
$txtstream.WriteLine("<table Border='0' cellpadding='1' cellspacing='1'>")
foreach($obj in $objs)
{
   $txtstream.WriteLine("<tr>")
   foreach($prop in $obj.Properties_)
   {
      $txtstream.WriteLine("<th>" + $prop.Name + "</th>")
   }
   $txtstream.WriteLine("</tr>")
   break
}
foreach($obj in $objs)
{
   $txtstream.WriteLine("<tr>")
   foreach($prop in $obj.Properties_)
   {
      $Name = $prop.Name
      $value = GetValue $Name $obj
      $txtstream.WriteLine("<td>" + $value + "</td>")
   }
   $txtstream.WriteLine("</tr>")
}
$txtstream.WriteLine("</table>")
$txtstream.WriteLine("</body>")
$txtstream.WriteLine("</html>")
$txtstream.Close()
```

Stylesheets

The difference between boring and oh, wow!

The stylesheets in Appendix A, were used to render these pages. If you find one you like, feel free to use it.

Report:

OrderID | CustomerID | EmployeeID | OrderDate | RequiredDate | ShippedDate | ShipVia | Freight | ShipName | ShipAddress | ShipCity | ShipRegion | ShipPostalCode | ShipCountry

Table

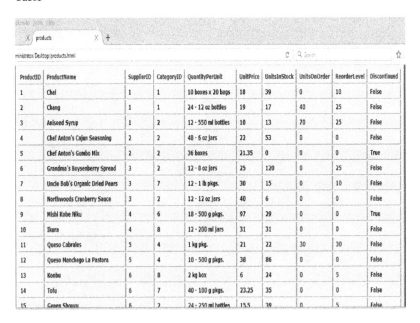

ProductID	ProductName	SupplierID	CategoryID	QuantityPerUnit	UnitPrice	UnitsInStock	UnitsOnOrder	ReorderLevel	Discontinued
1	Chai	1	1	10 boxes x 20 bags	18	39	0	10	False
2	Chang	1	1	24 - 12 oz bottles	19	17	40	25	False
3	Aniseed Syrup	1	2	12 - 550 ml bottles	10	13	70	25	False
4	Chef Anton's Cajun Seasoning	2	2	48 - 6 oz jars	22	53	0	0	False
5	Chef Anton's Gumbo Mix	2	2	36 boxes	21.35	0	0	0	True
6	Grandma's Boysenberry Spread	3	2	12 - 8 oz jars	25	120	0	25	False
7	Uncle Bob's Organic Dried Pears	3	7	12 - 1 lb pkgs.	30	15	0	10	False
8	Northwoods Cranberry Sauce	3	2	12 - 12 oz jars	40	6	0	0	False
9	Mishi Kobe Niku	4	6	18 - 500 g pkgs.	97	29	0	0	True
10	Ikura	4	8	12 - 200 ml jars	31	31	0	0	False
11	Queso Cabrales	5	4	1 kg pkg.	21	22	30	30	False
12	Queso Manchego La Pastora	5	4	10 - 500 g pkgs.	38	86	0	0	False
13	Konbu	6	8	2 kg box	6	24	0	5	False
14	Tofu	6	7	40 - 100 g pkgs.	23.25	35	0	0	False
15	Genen Shouyu	6	2	24 - 250 ml bottles	15.5	39	0	5	False

None:

Availability	BytesPerSector	Capabilities	CapabilityDescriptions	Caption	CompressionMethod	ConfigManagerErrorCode
	512	3, 4, 10	Random Access, Supports Writing, SMART Notification	OCZ REVODRIVE350 SCSI Disk Device		0
	512	3, 4	Random Access, Supports Writing	NVMe TOSHIBA-RD400		0
	512	3, 4, 10	Random Access, Supports Writing, SMART Notification	TOSHIBA DT01ACA200		0

Black and White

Colored:

AccountExpires	AuthorizationFlags	BadPasswordCount	Caption	CodePage	Comment	CountryCode	Description
			NT AUTHORITY\SYSTEM				Network login profile settings for SYSTEM on NT AUTHORITY
			NT AUTHORITY\LOCAL SERVICE				Network login profile settings for LOCAL SERVICE on NT AUTHORITY
			NT AUTHORITY\NETWORK SERVICE				Network login profile settings for NETWORK SERVICE on NT AUTHORITY
	0	0	Administrator	0	Built-in account for administering the computer/domain	0	Network login profile settings for on WIN-8J8LOAKM5YB
			NT SERVICE\SQLTELEMETRY				Network login profile settings for SQLTELEMETRY on NT SERVICE
			NT SERVICE\SQLTELEMETRY$30				Network login profile settings for SQLTELEMETRY$30 on NT SERVICE
			NT SERVICE\SQLTELEMETRY				Network login profile settings for SQLTELEMETRY on NT SERVICE
			NT SERVICE\MSSQLServerOLAPService				Network login profile settings for MSSQLServerOLAPService on NT SERVICE
			NT SERVICE\ReportServer				Network login profile settings for ReportServer on NT SERVICE
			NT SERVICE\MSSQLFDLauncher				Network login profile settings for MSSQLFDLauncher on NT SERVICE
			NT SERVICE\MSSQLLaunchpad				Network login profile settings for MSSQLLaunchpad on NT SERVICE
			NT SERVICE\MsDtsServer130				Network login profile settings for MsDtsServer130 on NT SERVICE
			NT SERVICE\MSSQLSERVER				Network login profile settings for MSSQLSERVER on NT SERVICE
			IIS APPPOOL\Classic .NET AppPool				Network login profile settings for Classic .NET AppPool on IIS APPPOOL
			IIS APPPOOL\.NET v4.5				Network login profile settings for .NET v4.5 on IIS APPPOOL
			IIS APPPOOL\.NET v2.0				Network login profile settings for .NET v2.0 on IIS APPPOOL
			IIS APPPOOL\.NET v4.5 Classic				Network login profile settings for .NET v4.5 Classic on IIS APPPOOL
			IIS APPPOOL\.NET v2.0 Classic				Network login profile settings for .NET v2.0 Classic on IIS APPPOOL

Oscillating:

Availability	BytesPerSector	Capabilities	CapabilityDescriptions	Caption	CompressionMethod	ConfigManagerErrorCode	ConfigManagerUserConfig
512	3, 4, 10	Random Access, Supports Writing, SMART Notification	OCZ REVODRIVE350 SCSI Disk Device		0		FALSE
512	3, 4	Random Access, Supports Writing	NVMe TOSHIBA-RD400		0		FALSE
512	3, 4, 10	Random Access, Supports Writing, SMART Notification	TOSHIBA DT01ACA200		0		FALSE

3D:

Shadow Box:

Shadow Box Single Line Vertical

82

BiosCharacteristics	7, 10, 11, 12, 15, 16, 17, 19, 23, 24, 25, 26, 27, 28, 29, 32, 33, 40, 42, 43, 48, 50, 58, 59, 64, 65, 66, 67, 68, 69, 70, 71, 72, 73, 74, 75, 76, 77, 78, 79
BIOSVersion	ALASKA - 1072009, 0504, American Megatrends - 5000C
BuildNumber	
Caption	0504
CodeSet	
CurrentLanguage	en|US|iso8859-1
Description	0504
IdentificationCode	
InstallableLanguages	8
InstallDate	
LanguageEdition	
ListOfLanguages	en|US|iso8859-1, fr|FR|iso8859-1, zh|CN|unicode, , , , ,
Manufacturer	American Megatrends Inc.
Name	0504
OtherTargetOS	
PrimaryBIOS	TRUE

Shadow Box Multi line Vertical

Availability			
BytesPerSector	512	512	512
Capabilities	3, 4, 10	3, 4	3, 4, 10
CapabilityDescriptions	Random Access, Supports Writing, SMART Notification	Random Access, Supports Writing	Random Access, Supports Writing, SMART Notification
Caption	OCZ REVODRIVE350 SCSI Disk Device	NVMe TOSHIBA-RD40	TOSHIBA DT01ACA200
CompressionMethod			
ConfigManagerErrorCode	0	0	0
ConfigManagerUserConfig	FALSE	FALSE	FALSE
CreationClassName	Win32_DiskDrive	Win32_DiskDrive	Win32_DiskDrive
DefaultBlockSize			
Description	Disk drive	Disk drive	Disk drive
DeviceID	\\.\PHYSICALDRIVE2	\\.\PHYSICALDRIVE1	\\.\PHYSICALDRIVE0
ErrorCleared			
ErrorDescription			
ErrorMethodology			
FirmwareRevision	2.80	SVCKA102	MX4OA3B0
Index	2	1	0

Stylesheets
Decorating your web pages

BELOW ARE SOME STYLESHEETS I COOKED UP THAT I LIKE AND THINK YOU MIGHT TOO. Don't worry I won't be offended if you take and modify to your hearts delight. Please do!

NONE

```
$txtstream.WriteLine("<style type='text/css'>")
$txtstream.WriteLine("th")
$txtstream.WriteLine("{")
$txtstream.WriteLine("    COLOR: white;")
$txtstream.WriteLine("}")
$txtstream.WriteLine("td")
$txtstream.WriteLine("{")
$txtstream.WriteLine("    COLOR: white;")
$txtstream.WriteLine("}")
$txtstream.WriteLine("</style>")
```

BLACK AND WHITE TEXT

```
$txtstream.WriteLine("<style type='text/css'>")
$txtstream.WriteLine("th")
$txtstream.WriteLine("{")
$txtstream.WriteLine("    COLOR: white;")
$txtstream.WriteLine("    BACKGROUND-COLOR: black;")
$txtstream.WriteLine("    FONT-FAMILY:font-family: Cambria, serif;")
```

```
$txtstream.WriteLine("    FONT-SIZE: 12px;")
$txtstream.WriteLine("    text-align: left;")
$txtstream.WriteLine("    white-Space: nowrap;")
$txtstream.WriteLine("}")
$txtstream.WriteLine("td")
$txtstream.WriteLine("{")
$txtstream.WriteLine("    COLOR: white;")
$txtstream.WriteLine("    BACKGROUND-COLOR: black;")
$txtstream.WriteLine("    FONT-FAMILY: font-family: Cambria, serif;")
$txtstream.WriteLine("    FONT-SIZE: 12px;")
$txtstream.WriteLine("    text-align: left;")
$txtstream.WriteLine("    white-Space: nowrap;")
$txtstream.WriteLine("}")
$txtstream.WriteLine("div")
$txtstream.WriteLine("{")
$txtstream.WriteLine("    COLOR: white;")
$txtstream.WriteLine("    BACKGROUND-COLOR: black;")
$txtstream.WriteLine("    FONT-FAMILY: font-family: Cambria, serif;")
$txtstream.WriteLine("    FONT-SIZE: 10px;")
$txtstream.WriteLine("    text-align: left;")
$txtstream.WriteLine("    white-Space: nowrap;")
$txtstream.WriteLine("}")
$txtstream.WriteLine("span")
$txtstream.WriteLine("{")
$txtstream.WriteLine("    COLOR: white;")
$txtstream.WriteLine("    BACKGROUND-COLOR: black;")
$txtstream.WriteLine("    FONT-FAMILY: font-family: Cambria, serif;")
$txtstream.WriteLine("    FONT-SIZE: 10px;")
$txtstream.WriteLine("    text-align: left;")
$txtstream.WriteLine("    white-Space: nowrap;")
$txtstream.WriteLine("    display:inline-block;")
$txtstream.WriteLine("    width: 100%;")
$txtstream.WriteLine("}")
$txtstream.WriteLine("textarea")
$txtstream.WriteLine("{")
$txtstream.WriteLine("    COLOR: white;")
$txtstream.WriteLine("    BACKGROUND-COLOR: black;")
$txtstream.WriteLine("    FONT-FAMILY: font-family: Cambria, serif;")
$txtstream.WriteLine("    FONT-SIZE: 10px;")
$txtstream.WriteLine("    text-align: left;")
$txtstream.WriteLine("    white-Space: nowrap;")
$txtstream.WriteLine("    width: 100%;")
$txtstream.WriteLine("}")
$txtstream.WriteLine("select")
$txtstream.WriteLine("{")
$txtstream.WriteLine("    COLOR: white;")
$txtstream.WriteLine("    BACKGROUND-COLOR: black;")
$txtstream.WriteLine("    FONT-FAMILY: font-family: Cambria, serif;")
$txtstream.WriteLine("    FONT-SIZE: 10px;")
$txtstream.WriteLine("    text-align: left;")
```

```
$txtstream.WriteLine("    white-Space: nowrap;")
$txtstream.WriteLine("    width: 100%;")
$txtstream.WriteLine("}")
$txtstream.WriteLine("input")
$txtstream.WriteLine("{")
$txtstream.WriteLine("    COLOR: white;")
$txtstream.WriteLine("    BACKGROUND-COLOR: black;")
$txtstream.WriteLine("    FONT-FAMILY: font-family: Cambria, serif;")
$txtstream.WriteLine("    FONT-SIZE: 12px;")
$txtstream.WriteLine("    text-align: left;")
$txtstream.WriteLine("    display:table-cell;")
$txtstream.WriteLine("    white-Space: nowrap;")
$txtstream.WriteLine("}")
$txtstream.WriteLine("h1 {")
$txtstream.WriteLine("color: antiquewhite;")
$txtstream.WriteLine("text-shadow: 1px 1px 1px black;")
$txtstream.WriteLine("padding: 3px;")
$txtstream.WriteLine("text-align: center;")
$txtstream.WriteLine("box-shadow: inset 2px 2px 5px rgba(0,0,0,0.5), inset -2px -2px 5px rgba(255,255,255,0.5)")
$txtstream.WriteLine("}")
$txtstream.WriteLine("</style>")
```

COLORED TEXT

```
$txtstream.WriteLine("<style type='text/css'>")
$txtstream.WriteLine("th")
$txtstream.WriteLine("{")
$txtstream.WriteLine("    COLOR: darkred;")
$txtstream.WriteLine("    BACKGROUND-COLOR: #eeeeee;")
$txtstream.WriteLine("    FONT-FAMILY:font-family: Cambria, serif;")
$txtstream.WriteLine("    FONT-SIZE: 12px;")
$txtstream.WriteLine("    text-align: left;")
$txtstream.WriteLine("    white-Space: nowrap;")
$txtstream.WriteLine("}")
$txtstream.WriteLine("td")
$txtstream.WriteLine("{")
$txtstream.WriteLine("    COLOR: navy;")
$txtstream.WriteLine("    BACKGROUND-COLOR: #eeeeee;")
$txtstream.WriteLine("    FONT-FAMILY: font-family: Cambria, serif;")
$txtstream.WriteLine("    FONT-SIZE: 12px;")
$txtstream.WriteLine("    text-align: left;")
$txtstream.WriteLine("    white-Space: nowrap;")
$txtstream.WriteLine("}")
$txtstream.WriteLine("div")
$txtstream.WriteLine("{")
$txtstream.WriteLine("    COLOR: white;")
$txtstream.WriteLine("    BACKGROUND-COLOR: navy;")
$txtstream.WriteLine("    FONT-FAMILY: font-family: Cambria, serif;")
$txtstream.WriteLine("    FONT-SIZE: 10px;")
```

```
$txtstream.WriteLine("   text-align: left;")
$txtstream.WriteLine("   white-Space: nowrap;")
$txtstream.WriteLine("}")
$txtstream.WriteLine("span")
$txtstream.WriteLine("{")
$txtstream.WriteLine("   COLOR: white;")
$txtstream.WriteLine("   BACKGROUND-COLOR: navy;")
$txtstream.WriteLine("   FONT-FAMILY: font-family: Cambria, serif;")
$txtstream.WriteLine("   FONT-SIZE: 10px;")
$txtstream.WriteLine("   text-align: left;")
$txtstream.WriteLine("   white-Space: nowrap;")
$txtstream.WriteLine("   display:inline-block;")
$txtstream.WriteLine("   width: 100%;")
$txtstream.WriteLine("}")
$txtstream.WriteLine("textarea")
$txtstream.WriteLine("{")
$txtstream.WriteLine("   COLOR: white;")
$txtstream.WriteLine("   BACKGROUND-COLOR: navy;")
$txtstream.WriteLine("   FONT-FAMILY: font-family: Cambria, serif;")
$txtstream.WriteLine("   FONT-SIZE: 10px;")
$txtstream.WriteLine("   text-align: left;")
$txtstream.WriteLine("   white-Space: nowrap;")
$txtstream.WriteLine("   width: 100%;")
$txtstream.WriteLine("}")
$txtstream.WriteLine("select")
$txtstream.WriteLine("{")
$txtstream.WriteLine("   COLOR: white;")
$txtstream.WriteLine("   BACKGROUND-COLOR: navy;")
$txtstream.WriteLine("   FONT-FAMILY: font-family: Cambria, serif;")
$txtstream.WriteLine("   FONT-SIZE: 10px;")
$txtstream.WriteLine("   text-align: left;")
$txtstream.WriteLine("   white-Space: nowrap;")
$txtstream.WriteLine("   width: 100%;")
$txtstream.WriteLine("}")
$txtstream.WriteLine("input")
$txtstream.WriteLine("{")
$txtstream.WriteLine("   COLOR: white;")
$txtstream.WriteLine("   BACKGROUND-COLOR: navy;")
$txtstream.WriteLine("   FONT-FAMILY: font-family: Cambria, serif;")
$txtstream.WriteLine("   FONT-SIZE: 12px;")
$txtstream.WriteLine("   text-align: left;")
$txtstream.WriteLine("   display:table-cell;")
$txtstream.WriteLine("   white-Space: nowrap;")
$txtstream.WriteLine("}")
$txtstream.WriteLine("h1 {")
$txtstream.WriteLine("color: antiquewhite;")
$txtstream.WriteLine("text-shadow: 1px 1px 1px black;")
$txtstream.WriteLine("padding: 3px;")
$txtstream.WriteLine("text-align: center;")
```

```
$txtstream.WriteLine("box-shadow: inset 2px 2px 5px rgba(0,0,0,0.5), inset -
2px -2px 5px rgba(255,255,255,0.5)")
    $txtstream.WriteLine("}")
    $txtstream.WriteLine("</style>")
```

OSCILLATING ROW COLORS

```
    $txtstream.WriteLine("<style>")
    $txtstream.WriteLine("th")
    $txtstream.WriteLine("{")
    $txtstream.WriteLine("    COLOR: white;")
    $txtstream.WriteLine("    BACKGROUND-COLOR: navy;")
    $txtstream.WriteLine("    FONT-FAMILY:font-family: Cambria, serif;")
    $txtstream.WriteLine("    FONT-SIZE: 12px;")
    $txtstream.WriteLine("    text-align: left;")
    $txtstream.WriteLine("    white-Space: nowrap;")
    $txtstream.WriteLine("}")
    $txtstream.WriteLine("td")
    $txtstream.WriteLine("{")
    $txtstream.WriteLine("    COLOR: navy;")
    $txtstream.WriteLine("    FONT-FAMILY: font-family: Cambria, serif;")
    $txtstream.WriteLine("    FONT-SIZE: 12px;")
    $txtstream.WriteLine("    text-align: left;")
    $txtstream.WriteLine("    white-Space: nowrap;")
    $txtstream.WriteLine("}")
    $txtstream.WriteLine("div")
    $txtstream.WriteLine("{")
    $txtstream.WriteLine("    COLOR: navy;")
    $txtstream.WriteLine("    FONT-FAMILY: font-family: Cambria, serif;")
    $txtstream.WriteLine("    FONT-SIZE: 12px;")
    $txtstream.WriteLine("    text-align: left;")
    $txtstream.WriteLine("    white-Space: nowrap;")
    $txtstream.WriteLine("}")
    $txtstream.WriteLine("span")
    $txtstream.WriteLine("{")
    $txtstream.WriteLine("    COLOR: navy;")
    $txtstream.WriteLine("    FONT-FAMILY: font-family: Cambria, serif;")
    $txtstream.WriteLine("    FONT-SIZE: 12px;")
    $txtstream.WriteLine("    text-align: left;")
    $txtstream.WriteLine("    white-Space: nowrap;")
    $txtstream.WriteLine("    width: 100%;")
    $txtstream.WriteLine("}")
    $txtstream.WriteLine("textarea")
    $txtstream.WriteLine("{")
    $txtstream.WriteLine("    COLOR: navy;")
    $txtstream.WriteLine("    FONT-FAMILY: font-family: Cambria, serif;")
    $txtstream.WriteLine("    FONT-SIZE: 12px;")
    $txtstream.WriteLine("    text-align: left;")
```

```
$txtstream.WriteLine("    white-Space: nowrap;")
$txtstream.WriteLine("    display:inline-block;")
$txtstream.WriteLine("    width: 100%;")
$txtstream.WriteLine("}")
$txtstream.WriteLine("select")
$txtstream.WriteLine("{")
$txtstream.WriteLine("    COLOR: navy;")
$txtstream.WriteLine("    FONT-FAMILY: font-family: Cambria, serif;")
$txtstream.WriteLine("    FONT-SIZE: 10px;")
$txtstream.WriteLine("    text-align: left;")
$txtstream.WriteLine("    white-Space: nowrap;")
$txtstream.WriteLine("    display:inline-block;")
$txtstream.WriteLine("    width: 100%;")
$txtstream.WriteLine("}")
$txtstream.WriteLine("input")
$txtstream.WriteLine("{")
$txtstream.WriteLine("    COLOR: navy;")
$txtstream.WriteLine("    FONT-FAMILY: font-family: Cambria, serif;")
$txtstream.WriteLine("    FONT-SIZE: 12px;")
$txtstream.WriteLine("    text-align: left;")
$txtstream.WriteLine("    display:table-cell;")
$txtstream.WriteLine("    white-Space: nowrap;")
$txtstream.WriteLine("}")
$txtstream.WriteLine("h1 {")
$txtstream.WriteLine("color: antiquewhite;")
$txtstream.WriteLine("text-shadow: 1px 1px 1px black;")
$txtstream.WriteLine("padding: 3px;")
$txtstream.WriteLine("text-align: center;")
$txtstream.WriteLine("box-shadow: inset 2px 2px 5px rgba(0,0,0,0.5), inset -2px -2px 5px rgba(255,255,255,0.5)")
$txtstream.WriteLine("}")
$txtstream.WriteLine("tr:nth-child(even){background-color:#f2f2f2;}")
$txtstream.WriteLine("tr:nth-child(odd){background-color:#cccccc; color:#f2f2f2;}")
$txtstream.WriteLine("</style>")
```

GHOST DECORATED

```
$txtstream.WriteLine("<style type='text/css'>")
$txtstream.WriteLine("th")
$txtstream.WriteLine("{")
$txtstream.WriteLine("    COLOR: black;")
$txtstream.WriteLine("    BACKGROUND-COLOR: white;")
$txtstream.WriteLine("    FONT-FAMILY:font-family: Cambria, serif;")
$txtstream.WriteLine("    FONT-SIZE: 12px;")
$txtstream.WriteLine("    text-align: left;")
$txtstream.WriteLine("    white-Space: nowrap;")
$txtstream.WriteLine("}")
$txtstream.WriteLine("td")
$txtstream.WriteLine("{")
```

```
$txtstream.WriteLine("    COLOR: black;")
$txtstream.WriteLine("    BACKGROUND-COLOR: white;")
$txtstream.WriteLine("    FONT-FAMILY: font-family: Cambria, serif;")
$txtstream.WriteLine("    FONT-SIZE: 12px;")
$txtstream.WriteLine("    text-align: left;")
$txtstream.WriteLine("    white-Space: nowrap;")
$txtstream.WriteLine("}")
$txtstream.WriteLine("div")
$txtstream.WriteLine("{")
$txtstream.WriteLine("    COLOR: black;")
$txtstream.WriteLine("    BACKGROUND-COLOR: white;")
$txtstream.WriteLine("    FONT-FAMILY: font-family: Cambria, serif;")
$txtstream.WriteLine("    FONT-SIZE: 10px;")
$txtstream.WriteLine("    text-align: left;")
$txtstream.WriteLine("    white-Space: nowrap;")
$txtstream.WriteLine("}")
$txtstream.WriteLine("span")
$txtstream.WriteLine("{")
$txtstream.WriteLine("    COLOR: black;")
$txtstream.WriteLine("    BACKGROUND-COLOR: white;")
$txtstream.WriteLine("    FONT-FAMILY: font-family: Cambria, serif;")
$txtstream.WriteLine("    FONT-SIZE: 10px;")
$txtstream.WriteLine("    text-align: left;")
$txtstream.WriteLine("    white-Space: nowrap;")
$txtstream.WriteLine("    display:inline-block;")
$txtstream.WriteLine("    width: 100%;")
$txtstream.WriteLine("}")
$txtstream.WriteLine("textarea")
$txtstream.WriteLine("{")
$txtstream.WriteLine("    COLOR: black;")
$txtstream.WriteLine("    BACKGROUND-COLOR: white;")
$txtstream.WriteLine("    FONT-FAMILY: font-family: Cambria, serif;")
$txtstream.WriteLine("    FONT-SIZE: 10px;")
$txtstream.WriteLine("    text-align: left;")
$txtstream.WriteLine("    white-Space: nowrap;")
$txtstream.WriteLine("    width: 100%;")
$txtstream.WriteLine("}")
$txtstream.WriteLine("select")
$txtstream.WriteLine("{")
$txtstream.WriteLine("    COLOR: black;")
$txtstream.WriteLine("    BACKGROUND-COLOR: white;")
$txtstream.WriteLine("    FONT-FAMILY: font-family: Cambria, serif;")
$txtstream.WriteLine("    FONT-SIZE: 10px;")
$txtstream.WriteLine("    text-align: left;")
$txtstream.WriteLine("    white-Space: nowrap;")
$txtstream.WriteLine("    width: 100%;")
$txtstream.WriteLine("}")
$txtstream.WriteLine("input")
$txtstream.WriteLine("{")
$txtstream.WriteLine("    COLOR: black;")
```

```
$txtstream.WriteLine("    BACKGROUND-COLOR: white;")
$txtstream.WriteLine("    FONT-FAMILY: font-family: Cambria, serif;")
$txtstream.WriteLine("    FONT-SIZE: 12px;")
$txtstream.WriteLine("    text-align: left;")
$txtstream.WriteLine("    display:table-cell;")
$txtstream.WriteLine("    white-Space: nowrap;")
$txtstream.WriteLine("}")
$txtstream.WriteLine("h1 {")
$txtstream.WriteLine("color: antiquewhite;")
$txtstream.WriteLine("text-shadow: 1px 1px 1px black;")
$txtstream.WriteLine("padding: 3px;")
$txtstream.WriteLine("text-align: center;")
$txtstream.WriteLine("box-shadow: inset 2px 2px 5px rgba(0,0,0,0.5), inset -
2px -2px 5px rgba(255,255,255,0.5)")
$txtstream.WriteLine("}")
$txtstream.WriteLine("</style>")
```

3D

```
$txtstream.WriteLine("<style type='text/css'>")
$txtstream.WriteLine("body")
$txtstream.WriteLine("{")
$txtstream.WriteLine("    PADDING-RIGHT: 0px;")
$txtstream.WriteLine("    PADDING-LEFT: 0px;")
$txtstream.WriteLine("    PADDING-BOTTOM: 0px;")
$txtstream.WriteLine("    MARGIN: 0px;")
$txtstream.WriteLine("    COLOR: #333;")
$txtstream.WriteLine("    PADDING-TOP: 0px;")
$txtstream.WriteLine("        FONT-FAMILY: verdana, arial, helvetica, sans-
serif;")
$txtstream.WriteLine("}")
$txtstream.WriteLine("table")
$txtstream.WriteLine("{")
$txtstream.WriteLine("    BORDER-RIGHT: #999999 3px solid;")
$txtstream.WriteLine("    PADDING-RIGHT: 6px;")
$txtstream.WriteLine("    PADDING-LEFT: 6px;")
$txtstream.WriteLine("    FONT-WEIGHT: Bold;")
$txtstream.WriteLine("    FONT-SIZE: 14px;")
$txtstream.WriteLine("    PADDING-BOTTOM: 6px;")
$txtstream.WriteLine("    COLOR: Peru;")
$txtstream.WriteLine("    LINE-HEIGHT: 14px;")
$txtstream.WriteLine("    PADDING-TOP: 6px;")
$txtstream.WriteLine("    BORDER-BOTTOM: #999 1px solid;")
$txtstream.WriteLine("    BACKGROUND-COLOR: #eeeeee;")
$txtstream.WriteLine("        FONT-FAMILY: verdana, arial, helvetica, sans-
serif;")
$txtstream.WriteLine("    FONT-SIZE: 12px;")
$txtstream.WriteLine("}")
$txtstream.WriteLine("th")
```

```
$txtstream.WriteLine("{")
$txtstream.WriteLine("   BORDER-RIGHT: #999999 3px solid;")
$txtstream.WriteLine("   PADDING-RIGHT: 6px;")
$txtstream.WriteLine("   PADDING-LEFT: 6px;")
$txtstream.WriteLine("   FONT-WEIGHT: Bold;")
$txtstream.WriteLine("   FONT-SIZE: 14px;")
$txtstream.WriteLine("   PADDING-BOTTOM: 6px;")
$txtstream.WriteLine("   COLOR: darkred;")
$txtstream.WriteLine("   LINE-HEIGHT: 14px;")
$txtstream.WriteLine("   PADDING-TOP: 6px;")
$txtstream.WriteLine("   BORDER-BOTTOM: #999 1px solid;")
$txtstream.WriteLine("   BACKGROUND-COLOR: #eeeeee;")
$txtstream.WriteLine("   FONT-FAMILY:font-family: Cambria, serif;")
$txtstream.WriteLine("   FONT-SIZE: 12px;")
$txtstream.WriteLine("   text-align: left;")
$txtstream.WriteLine("   white-Space: nowrap;")
$txtstream.WriteLine("}")
$txtstream.WriteLine(".th")
$txtstream.WriteLine("{")
$txtstream.WriteLine("   BORDER-RIGHT: #999999 2px solid;")
$txtstream.WriteLine("   PADDING-RIGHT: 6px;")
$txtstream.WriteLine("   PADDING-LEFT: 6px;")
$txtstream.WriteLine("   FONT-WEIGHT: Bold;")
$txtstream.WriteLine("   PADDING-BOTTOM: 6px;")
$txtstream.WriteLine("   COLOR: black;")
$txtstream.WriteLine("   PADDING-TOP: 6px;")
$txtstream.WriteLine("   BORDER-BOTTOM: #999 2px solid;")
$txtstream.WriteLine("   BACKGROUND-COLOR: #eeeeee;")
$txtstream.WriteLine("   FONT-FAMILY: font-family: Cambria, serif;")
$txtstream.WriteLine("   FONT-SIZE: 10px;")
$txtstream.WriteLine("   text-align: right;")
$txtstream.WriteLine("   white-Space: nowrap;")
$txtstream.WriteLine("}")
$txtstream.WriteLine("td")
$txtstream.WriteLine("{")
$txtstream.WriteLine("   BORDER-RIGHT: #999999 3px solid;")
$txtstream.WriteLine("   PADDING-RIGHT: 6px;")
$txtstream.WriteLine("   PADDING-LEFT: 6px;")
$txtstream.WriteLine("   FONT-WEIGHT: Normal;")
$txtstream.WriteLine("   PADDING-BOTTOM: 6px;")
$txtstream.WriteLine("   COLOR: navy;")
$txtstream.WriteLine("   LINE-HEIGHT: 14px;")
$txtstream.WriteLine("   PADDING-TOP: 6px;")
$txtstream.WriteLine("   BORDER-BOTTOM: #999 1px solid;")
$txtstream.WriteLine("   BACKGROUND-COLOR: #eeeeee;")
$txtstream.WriteLine("   FONT-FAMILY: font-family: Cambria, serif;")
$txtstream.WriteLine("   FONT-SIZE: 12px;")
$txtstream.WriteLine("   text-align: left;")
$txtstream.WriteLine("   white-Space: nowrap;")
$txtstream.WriteLine("}")
```

```
$txtstream.WriteLine("div")
$txtstream.WriteLine("{")
$txtstream.WriteLine("    BORDER-RIGHT: #999999 3px solid;")
$txtstream.WriteLine("    PADDING-RIGHT: 6px;")
$txtstream.WriteLine("    PADDING-LEFT: 6px;")
$txtstream.WriteLine("    FONT-WEIGHT: Normal;")
$txtstream.WriteLine("    PADDING-BOTTOM: 6px;")
$txtstream.WriteLine("    COLOR: white;")
$txtstream.WriteLine("    PADDING-TOP: 6px;")
$txtstream.WriteLine("    BORDER-BOTTOM: #999 1px solid;")
$txtstream.WriteLine("    BACKGROUND-COLOR: navy;")
$txtstream.WriteLine("    FONT-FAMILY: font-family: Cambria, serif;")
$txtstream.WriteLine("    FONT-SIZE: 10px;")
$txtstream.WriteLine("    text-align: left;")
$txtstream.WriteLine("    white-Space: nowrap;")
$txtstream.WriteLine("}")
$txtstream.WriteLine("span")
$txtstream.WriteLine("{")
$txtstream.WriteLine("    BORDER-RIGHT: #999999 3px solid;")
$txtstream.WriteLine("    PADDING-RIGHT: 3px;")
$txtstream.WriteLine("    PADDING-LEFT: 3px;")
$txtstream.WriteLine("    FONT-WEIGHT: Normal;")
$txtstream.WriteLine("    PADDING-BOTTOM: 3px;")
$txtstream.WriteLine("    COLOR: white;")
$txtstream.WriteLine("    PADDING-TOP: 3px;")
$txtstream.WriteLine("    BORDER-BOTTOM: #999 1px solid;")
$txtstream.WriteLine("    BACKGROUND-COLOR: navy;")
$txtstream.WriteLine("    FONT-FAMILY: font-family: Cambria, serif;")
$txtstream.WriteLine("    FONT-SIZE: 10px;")
$txtstream.WriteLine("    text-align: left;")
$txtstream.WriteLine("    white-Space: nowrap;")
$txtstream.WriteLine("    display:inline-block;")
$txtstream.WriteLine("    width: 100%;")
$txtstream.WriteLine("}")
$txtstream.WriteLine("textarea")
$txtstream.WriteLine("{")
$txtstream.WriteLine("    BORDER-RIGHT: #999999 3px solid;")
$txtstream.WriteLine("    PADDING-RIGHT: 3px;")
$txtstream.WriteLine("    PADDING-LEFT: 3px;")
$txtstream.WriteLine("    FONT-WEIGHT: Normal;")
$txtstream.WriteLine("    PADDING-BOTTOM: 3px;")
$txtstream.WriteLine("    COLOR: white;")
$txtstream.WriteLine("    PADDING-TOP: 3px;")
$txtstream.WriteLine("    BORDER-BOTTOM: #999 1px solid;")
$txtstream.WriteLine("    BACKGROUND-COLOR: navy;")
$txtstream.WriteLine("    FONT-FAMILY: font-family: Cambria, serif;")
$txtstream.WriteLine("    FONT-SIZE: 10px;")
$txtstream.WriteLine("    text-align: left;")
$txtstream.WriteLine("    white-Space: nowrap;")
$txtstream.WriteLine("    width: 100%;")
```

```
$txtstream.WriteLine("}")
$txtstream.WriteLine("select")
$txtstream.WriteLine("{")
$txtstream.WriteLine("   BORDER-RIGHT: #999999 3px solid;")
$txtstream.WriteLine("   PADDING-RIGHT: 6px;")
$txtstream.WriteLine("   PADDING-LEFT: 6px;")
$txtstream.WriteLine("   FONT-WEIGHT: Normal;")
$txtstream.WriteLine("   PADDING-BOTTOM: 6px;")
$txtstream.WriteLine("   COLOR: white;")
$txtstream.WriteLine("   PADDING-TOP: 6px;")
$txtstream.WriteLine("   BORDER-BOTTOM: #999 1px solid;")
$txtstream.WriteLine("   BACKGROUND-COLOR: navy;")
$txtstream.WriteLine("   FONT-FAMILY: font-family: Cambria, serif;")
$txtstream.WriteLine("   FONT-SIZE: 10px;")
$txtstream.WriteLine("   text-align: left;")
$txtstream.WriteLine("   white-Space: nowrap;")
$txtstream.WriteLine("   width: 100%;")
$txtstream.WriteLine("}")
$txtstream.WriteLine("input")
$txtstream.WriteLine("{")
$txtstream.WriteLine("   BORDER-RIGHT: #999999 3px solid;")
$txtstream.WriteLine("   PADDING-RIGHT: 3px;")
$txtstream.WriteLine("   PADDING-LEFT: 3px;")
$txtstream.WriteLine("   FONT-WEIGHT: Bold;")
$txtstream.WriteLine("   PADDING-BOTTOM: 3px;")
$txtstream.WriteLine("   COLOR: white;")
$txtstream.WriteLine("   PADDING-TOP: 3px;")
$txtstream.WriteLine("   BORDER-BOTTOM: #999 1px solid;")
$txtstream.WriteLine("   BACKGROUND-COLOR: navy;")
$txtstream.WriteLine("   FONT-FAMILY: font-family: Cambria, serif;")
$txtstream.WriteLine("   FONT-SIZE: 12px;")
$txtstream.WriteLine("   text-align: left;")
$txtstream.WriteLine("   display:table-cell;")
$txtstream.WriteLine("   white-Space: nowrap;")
$txtstream.WriteLine("   width: 100%;")
$txtstream.WriteLine("}")
$txtstream.WriteLine("h1 {")
$txtstream.WriteLine("color: antiquewhite;")
$txtstream.WriteLine("text-shadow: 1px 1px 1px black;")
$txtstream.WriteLine("padding: 3px;")
$txtstream.WriteLine("text-align: center;")
$txtstream.WriteLine("box-shadow: inset 2px 2px 5px rgba(0,0,0,0.5), inset -2px -2px 5px rgba(255,255,255,0.5)")
$txtstream.WriteLine("}")
$txtstream.WriteLine("</style>")
```

SHADOW BOX

```
$txtstream.WriteLine("<style type='text/css'>")
```

```
$txtstream.WriteLine("body")
$txtstream.WriteLine("{")
$txtstream.WriteLine("    PADDING-RIGHT: 0px;")
$txtstream.WriteLine("    PADDING-LEFT: 0px;")
$txtstream.WriteLine("    PADDING-BOTTOM: 0px;")
$txtstream.WriteLine("    MARGIN: 0px;")
$txtstream.WriteLine("    COLOR: #333;")
$txtstream.WriteLine("    PADDING-TOP: 0px;")
$txtstream.WriteLine("    FONT-FAMILY: verdana, arial, helvetica, sans-serif;")
$txtstream.WriteLine("}")
$txtstream.WriteLine("table")
$txtstream.WriteLine("{")
$txtstream.WriteLine("    BORDER-RIGHT: #999999 1px solid;")
$txtstream.WriteLine("    PADDING-RIGHT: 1px;")
$txtstream.WriteLine("    PADDING-LEFT: 1px;")
$txtstream.WriteLine("    PADDING-BOTTOM: 1px;")
$txtstream.WriteLine("    LINE-HEIGHT: 8px;")
$txtstream.WriteLine("    PADDING-TOP: 1px;")
$txtstream.WriteLine("    BORDER-BOTTOM: #999 1px solid;")
$txtstream.WriteLine("    BACKGROUND-COLOR: #eeeeee;")
$txtstream.WriteLine("    filter:progid:DXImageTransform.Microsoft.Shadow(color='silver',    Direction=135, Strength=16)")
$txtstream.WriteLine("}")
$txtstream.WriteLine("th")
$txtstream.WriteLine("{")
$txtstream.WriteLine("    BORDER-RIGHT: #999999 3px solid;")
$txtstream.WriteLine("    PADDING-RIGHT: 6px;")
$txtstream.WriteLine("    PADDING-LEFT: 6px;")
$txtstream.WriteLine("    FONT-WEIGHT: Bold;")
$txtstream.WriteLine("    FONT-SIZE: 14px;")
$txtstream.WriteLine("    PADDING-BOTTOM: 6px;")
$txtstream.WriteLine("    COLOR: darkred;")
$txtstream.WriteLine("    LINE-HEIGHT: 14px;")
$txtstream.WriteLine("    PADDING-TOP: 6px;")
$txtstream.WriteLine("    BORDER-BOTTOM: #999 1px solid;")
$txtstream.WriteLine("    BACKGROUND-COLOR: #eeeeee;")
$txtstream.WriteLine("    FONT-FAMILY: font-family: Cambria, serif;")
$txtstream.WriteLine("    FONT-SIZE: 12px;")
$txtstream.WriteLine("    text-align: left;")
$txtstream.WriteLine("    white-Space: nowrap;")
$txtstream.WriteLine("}")
$txtstream.WriteLine(".th")
$txtstream.WriteLine("{")
$txtstream.WriteLine("    BORDER-RIGHT: #999999 2px solid;")
$txtstream.WriteLine("    PADDING-RIGHT: 6px;")
$txtstream.WriteLine("    PADDING-LEFT: 6px;")
$txtstream.WriteLine("    FONT-WEIGHT: Bold;")
$txtstream.WriteLine("    PADDING-BOTTOM: 6px;")
```

```
$txtstream.WriteLine("    COLOR: black;")
$txtstream.WriteLine("    PADDING-TOP: 6px;")
$txtstream.WriteLine("    BORDER-BOTTOM: #999 2px solid;")
$txtstream.WriteLine("    BACKGROUND-COLOR: #eeeeee;")
$txtstream.WriteLine("    FONT-FAMILY: font-family: Cambria, serif;")
$txtstream.WriteLine("    FONT-SIZE: 10px;")
$txtstream.WriteLine("    text-align: right;")
$txtstream.WriteLine("    white-Space: nowrap;")
$txtstream.WriteLine("}")
$txtstream.WriteLine("td")
$txtstream.WriteLine("{")
$txtstream.WriteLine("    BORDER-RIGHT: #999999 3px solid;")
$txtstream.WriteLine("    PADDING-RIGHT: 6px;")
$txtstream.WriteLine("    PADDING-LEFT: 6px;")
$txtstream.WriteLine("    FONT-WEIGHT: Normal;")
$txtstream.WriteLine("    PADDING-BOTTOM: 6px;")
$txtstream.WriteLine("    COLOR: navy;")
$txtstream.WriteLine("    LINE-HEIGHT: 14px;")
$txtstream.WriteLine("    PADDING-TOP: 6px;")
$txtstream.WriteLine("    BORDER-BOTTOM: #999 1px solid;")
$txtstream.WriteLine("    BACKGROUND-COLOR: #eeeeee;")
$txtstream.WriteLine("    FONT-FAMILY: font-family: Cambria, serif;")
$txtstream.WriteLine("    FONT-SIZE: 12px;")
$txtstream.WriteLine("    text-align: left;")
$txtstream.WriteLine("    white-Space: nowrap;")
$txtstream.WriteLine("}")
$txtstream.WriteLine("div")
$txtstream.WriteLine("{")
$txtstream.WriteLine("    BORDER-RIGHT: #999999 3px solid;")
$txtstream.WriteLine("    PADDING-RIGHT: 6px;")
$txtstream.WriteLine("    PADDING-LEFT: 6px;")
$txtstream.WriteLine("    FONT-WEIGHT: Normal;")
$txtstream.WriteLine("    PADDING-BOTTOM: 6px;")
$txtstream.WriteLine("    COLOR: white;")
$txtstream.WriteLine("    PADDING-TOP: 6px;")
$txtstream.WriteLine("    BORDER-BOTTOM: #999 1px solid;")
$txtstream.WriteLine("    BACKGROUND-COLOR: navy;")
$txtstream.WriteLine("    FONT-FAMILY: font-family: Cambria, serif;")
$txtstream.WriteLine("    FONT-SIZE: 10px;")
$txtstream.WriteLine("    text-align: left;")
$txtstream.WriteLine("    white-Space: nowrap;")
$txtstream.WriteLine("}")
$txtstream.WriteLine("span")
$txtstream.WriteLine("{")
$txtstream.WriteLine("    BORDER-RIGHT: #999999 3px solid;")
$txtstream.WriteLine("    PADDING-RIGHT: 3px;")
$txtstream.WriteLine("    PADDING-LEFT: 3px;")
$txtstream.WriteLine("    FONT-WEIGHT: Normal;")
$txtstream.WriteLine("    PADDING-BOTTOM: 3px;")
$txtstream.WriteLine("    COLOR: white;")
```

```
$txtstream.WriteLine("    PADDING-TOP: 3px;")
$txtstream.WriteLine("    BORDER-BOTTOM: #999 1px solid;")
$txtstream.WriteLine("    BACKGROUND-COLOR: navy;")
$txtstream.WriteLine("    FONT-FAMILY: font-family: Cambria, serif;")
$txtstream.WriteLine("    FONT-SIZE: 10px;")
$txtstream.WriteLine("    text-align: left;")
$txtstream.WriteLine("    white-Space: nowrap;")
$txtstream.WriteLine("    display: inline-block;")
$txtstream.WriteLine("    width: 100%;")
$txtstream.WriteLine("}")
$txtstream.WriteLine("textarea")
$txtstream.WriteLine("{")
$txtstream.WriteLine("    BORDER-RIGHT: #999999 3px solid;")
$txtstream.WriteLine("    PADDING-RIGHT: 3px;")
$txtstream.WriteLine("    PADDING-LEFT: 3px;")
$txtstream.WriteLine("    FONT-WEIGHT: Normal;")
$txtstream.WriteLine("    PADDING-BOTTOM: 3px;")
$txtstream.WriteLine("    COLOR: white;")
$txtstream.WriteLine("    PADDING-TOP: 3px;")
$txtstream.WriteLine("    BORDER-BOTTOM: #999 1px solid;")
$txtstream.WriteLine("    BACKGROUND-COLOR: navy;")
$txtstream.WriteLine("    FONT-FAMILY: font-family: Cambria, serif;")
$txtstream.WriteLine("    FONT-SIZE: 10px;")
$txtstream.WriteLine("    text-align: left;")
$txtstream.WriteLine("    white-Space: nowrap;")
$txtstream.WriteLine("    width: 100%;")
$txtstream.WriteLine("}")
$txtstream.WriteLine("select")
$txtstream.WriteLine("{")
$txtstream.WriteLine("    BORDER-RIGHT: #999999 3px solid;")
$txtstream.WriteLine("    PADDING-RIGHT: 6px;")
$txtstream.WriteLine("    PADDING-LEFT: 6px;")
$txtstream.WriteLine("    FONT-WEIGHT: Normal;")
$txtstream.WriteLine("    PADDING-BOTTOM: 6px;")
$txtstream.WriteLine("    COLOR: white;")
$txtstream.WriteLine("    PADDING-TOP: 6px;")
$txtstream.WriteLine("    BORDER-BOTTOM: #999 1px solid;")
$txtstream.WriteLine("    BACKGROUND-COLOR: navy;")
$txtstream.WriteLine("    FONT-FAMILY: font-family: Cambria, serif;")
$txtstream.WriteLine("    FONT-SIZE: 10px;")
$txtstream.WriteLine("    text-align: left;")
$txtstream.WriteLine("    white-Space: nowrap;")
$txtstream.WriteLine("    width: 100%;")
$txtstream.WriteLine("}")
$txtstream.WriteLine("input")
$txtstream.WriteLine("{")
$txtstream.WriteLine("    BORDER-RIGHT: #999999 3px solid;")
$txtstream.WriteLine("    PADDING-RIGHT: 3px;")
$txtstream.WriteLine("    PADDING-LEFT: 3px;")
$txtstream.WriteLine("    FONT-WEIGHT: Bold;")
```

```
$txtstream.WriteLine("    PADDING-BOTTOM: 3px;")
$txtstream.WriteLine("    COLOR: white;")
$txtstream.WriteLine("    PADDING-TOP: 3px;")
$txtstream.WriteLine("    BORDER-BOTTOM: #999 1px solid;")
$txtstream.WriteLine("    BACKGROUND-COLOR: navy;")
$txtstream.WriteLine("    FONT-FAMILY: font-family: Cambria, serif;")
$txtstream.WriteLine("    FONT-SIZE: 12px;")
$txtstream.WriteLine("    text-align: left;")
$txtstream.WriteLine("    display: table-cell;")
$txtstream.WriteLine("    white-Space: nowrap;")
$txtstream.WriteLine("    width: 100%;")
$txtstream.WriteLine("}")
$txtstream.WriteLine("h1 {")
$txtstream.WriteLine("color: antiquewhite;")
$txtstream.WriteLine("text-shadow: 1px 1px 1px black;")
$txtstream.WriteLine("padding: 3px;")
$txtstream.WriteLine("text-align: center;")
$txtstream.WriteLine("box-shadow: inset 2px 2px 5px rgba(0,0,0,0.5), inset -
2px -2px 5px rgba(255,255,255,0.5)")
$txtstream.WriteLine("}")
$txtstream.WriteLine("</style>")
```

www.ingramcontent.com/pod-product-compliance
Lightning Source LLC
Chambersburg PA
CBHW070848070326
40690CB00009B/1747